ARTHUR MILLER

A View from the Bridge

with commentary and notes by
STEPHEN MARINO

Series Editor: Enoch Brater

METHUEN DRAMA

Methuen Drama Student Edition

10 9 8 7 6 5 4 3 2 1

This edition first published in the United Kingdom in 2010 by
Methuen Drama
A & C Black Publishers Limited
36 Soho Square
London W1D 3QY
www.methuendrama.com

Chronology of Arthur Miller by Enoch Brater, with grateful thanks to the Arthur Miller
Society for permission to draw on their 'Brief Chronology of Arthur Miller's Life and
Works'

A CIP catalogue record for this book is available from the British Library

ISBN 978 1 408 10840 6

Commentary and notes typeset by SX Composing DTP, Rayleigh, Essex
Playtext typeset by Country Setting, Kingsdown, Kent
Printed and bound in Great Britain by CPI Cox & Wyman, Reading, Berkshire

Contents

Arthur Miller: 1915–2005

1915   17 October: Arthur Asher Miller born in New York City, the second of Isidore (Izzy) and Augusta (Gussie) Barnett Miller's three children. His brother Kermit born in 1912, sister Joan 1922.

1920–   Attends PS 24 in Harlem, then an upper-middle-
28   class Jewish neighbourhood, where his mother went to the same school. The family lives in an apartment overlooking Central Park on the top floor of a six-storey building at 45 West 110th Street, between Lenox and Fifth Avenues. Takes piano lessons, goes to Hebrew school and ice-skates in the park. His Barnett grandparents are nearby on West 118th Street. In summers the extended family rents a bungalow in Far Rockaway. Sees his first play in 1923, a melodrama at the Schubert Theatre.

1928   His father's successful manufacturing business in the Garment District, the Miltex Coat and Suit Company, with as many as 800 workers, begins to see hard times faced with the looming Depression. The family moves from Manhattan to rural Brooklyn, where they live at 1350 East 3rd Street, near Avenue M, in the same neighbourhood as his mother's two sisters, Annie Newman and Esther Balsam. Miller plants a pear tree in the backyard ('All I knew was cousins'). Celebrates his bar-mitzvah at the Avenue M Temple.

1930   Transfers from James Madison High School where he is reassigned to the newly built Abraham Lincoln High School on Ocean Parkway. Plays in the football team and injures his leg in a serious accident that will later excuse him from active military service. Academic record unimpressive, and he fails geometry twice.

1931   Early-morning delivery boy for a local bakery before going off to school; forced to stop when his bicycle is stolen. Works for his father during the summer vacation.

1933   Graduates from Abraham Lincoln High School and registers for night school at City College. He leaves after two weeks ('I just couldn't stay awake').

1933–   Earns $15 a week as a clerk for Chadwick-

34   Delamater, an automobile-parts warehouse in a run-
down section of Manhattan that will later become the site
for the Lincoln Center for the Performing Arts. He is the
only Jewish employee, and experiences virulent anti-
Semitism for the first time.

1934   Writes to the Dean of the University of Michigan to
appeal against his second rejection and says he has
become a 'much more serious fellow' ('I still can't believe
they let me in'). Travels by bus to Ann Arbor for the
autumn semester, with plans to study journalism because
'Michigan was one of the few places that took writing
seriously'. Lives in a rooming house on South Division
Street and joins the *Michigan Daily* as reporter and night
editor; takes a non-speaking part in a student production
of Shakespeare's *King Henry VIII*. Moves to an attic room
at 411 North State Street and works part-time in an off-
campus laboratory feeding past-prime vegetables to
thousands of mice.

1936   Writes his first play, *No Villain*, in six days during semester
break and receives a Hopwood Award in Drama for $250
using the pseudonym 'Beyoum'. Changes his major to
English.

1937   Enrols in Professor Kenneth T. Rowe's playwriting class.
Rewrites *No Villain* as *They Too Arise* and receives a major
award of $1,250 from the Theatre Guild's Bureau of New
Plays (Thomas Lanier – later Tennessee – Williams was
another winner in the same competition). *They Too Arise* is
produced by the B'nai Brith Hillel Players in Detroit and
at the Lydia Mendelssohn Theatre in Ann Arbor.
Receives a second Hopwood Award for *Honors at Dawn*
when Susan Glaspell is one of the judges. Contributes to
The Gargoyle, the student humour magazine. Drives his
college friend Ralph Neaphus east to join the Abraham
Lincoln Brigade in the Spanish Civil War, but decides not
to go with him. Months later Neaphus, twenty-three, was
dead.

1938   Composes a prison play, *The Great Disobedience*, and revises
They Too Arise as *The Grass Still Grows*. Graduates from the
University of Michigan with a BA in English. Joins the
Federal Theater Project in New York to write radio plays
and scripts.

1939   The Federal Theater Project is shut down by conservative
forces in Congress, and Miller goes on relief. Writes *Listen*

My Children and *You're Next* with his friend and fellow
Michigan alumnus, Norman Rosten. *William Ireland's
Confession* is broadcast on the Columbia Workshop.

1940   Marries Mary Grace Slattery, his college sweetheart at
the University of Michigan. They move into a small
apartment at 62 Montague Street in Brooklyn Heights.
Writes *The Golden Years*, a play about Montezuma, Cortez,
and the European conquest and corruption of Mexico.
The Pussycat and the Plumber Who Was a Man airs on CBS
Radio. Makes a trip to North Carolina to collect dialect
speech for the Folk Division of the Library of Congress.

1941–   Works as a shipfitter's helper on the night shift at the
43   Brooklyn Navy Yard repairing battle-scarred war vessels
from the North Atlantic fleet. Finishes additional radio
plays, including *The Eagle's Nest* and *The Four Freedoms*.
Completes *The Half-Bridge*. The one-act *That They May Win*
is produced in New York.

1944   Daughter Jane is born. Prepares Ferenc Molnar's *The
Guardsman* and Jane Austen's *Pride and Prejudice* for radio
adaptation, and continues his own writing for the
medium. Tours army camps in preparation for the draft
of a screenplay called *The Story of G.I. Joe*, based on news
reports written by the popular war correspondent Ernie
Pyle (withdraws from the project when his role as author
is compromised). Publishes *Situation Normal ...*, a book
about this experience that highlights the real challenges
returning soldiers encountered on re-entering civilian life.
Dedicates the book to his brother, 'Lieutenant Kermit
Miller, United States Infantry', a war hero. *The Man Who
Had All the Luck* opens on Broadway but closes after six
performances, including two previews. The play receives
the Theater Guild National Award.

1945   Publishes *Focus*, a novel about anti-Semitism and moral
blindness set in and around New York. His article
'Should Ezra Pound Be Shot?' appears in *New Masses*.

1946   Adapts *Three Men on a Horse* by George Abbott and John
C. Holm for radio.

1947   *All My Sons* opens in New York and receives the New
York Drama Critics' Circle Award; the Donaldson Award
and the first Tony Award for best author. His son Robert
is born. Moves with his family to a house he purchases at
31 Grace Court in Brooklyn Heights. Also buys a new
car, a Studebaker, and a farmhouse in Roxbury,

Connecticut. Writes the article 'Subsidized Theater' for the *New York Times*.

1948   Builds by himself a small studio on his Connecticut property where he writes *Death of a Salesman*. Edward G. Robinson and Burt Lancaster star in the film version of *All My Sons*.

1949   *Death of a Salesman*, starring Lee J. Cobb, Arthur Kennedy, Cameron Mitchell and Mildred Dunnock opens at the Morosco Theatre in New York on 10 February. Directed by Elia Kazan with designs by Jo Mielziner, it wins the New York Drama Critics' Circle Award, the Donaldson Prize, the Antoinette Perry Award, the Theatre Club Award and the Pulitzer Prize. His essay 'Tragedy and the Common Man' is printed in the *New York Times*. Attends the pro-Soviet Cultural and Scientific Conference for World Peace at the Waldorf-Astoria Hotel to chair a panel with Clifford Odets and Dimitri Shostakovich.

1950   Adaptation of Henrik Ibsen's *An Enemy of the People* produced on Broadway starring Fredric March and Florence Henderson ('I have made no secret of my early love for Ibsen's work'). First sound recording of *Death of a Salesman*. *The Hook*, a film script about graft and corruption in the closed world of longshoremen in the Red Hook section of Brooklyn, fails to reach production after backers yield to pressure from the House Committee on Un-American Activities. *On the Waterfront*, the Budd Schulberg–Elia Kazan collaboration featuring Marlon Brando, changes the setting to Hoboken, New Jersey, but is developed from the same concept, and is released four years later.

1951   Meets Marilyn Monroe. Fredric March in the role of Willy Loman for Columbia Pictures in the first film version of *Death of a Salesman*. Joseph Buloff translates the play into Yiddish; his production runs in New York and introduces Miller's play to Buenos Aires.

1952   Drives to Salem, Massachusetts, and visits the Historical Society, where he reads documents and researches the material he will use in *The Crucible*. Breaks with Kazan over the director's cooperation with HUAC.

1953   *The Crucible* wins the Donaldson Award and the Antoinette Perry Award when it opens in New York at the Martin Beck Theatre. Directs *All My Sons* for the Arden, Delaware, Summer Theatre.

1954   US State Department denies Miller a passport to attend
the Belgian premiere of *The Crucible* in Brussels ('I wasn't
embarrassed for myself; I was embarrassed for my
country'). NBC broadcasts the first radio production of
Death of a Salesman. Mingei Theater stages first Japanese
translation of *Salesman* in Tokyo, where the play is
received as a cautionary tale about the 'salaryman'.

1955   The one-act version of *A View from the Bridge* opens in New
York on a double-bill with *A Memory of Two Mondays*.
HUAC pressurises city officials to withdraw permission
for Miller to make a film about juvenile delinquency set in
New York.

1956   Lives in Nevada for six weeks in order to divorce Mary
Slattery. Marries Marilyn Monroe. Subpoenaed to appear
before HUAC on 21 June, he refuses to name names.
Accepts an honorary degree as Doctor of Humane Letters
from his alma mater, the University of Michigan. Jean-Paul
Sartre writes screenplay for French adaptation of *The
Crucible*, called *Les Sorcieres de Salem*; the film stars Yves
Montand and Simone Signoret. Travels with Monroe to
England, where he meets Laurence Olivier, her co-star in
The Prince and the Showgirl. Peter Brook directs revised two-
act version of *A View from the Bridge* in London at the New
Watergate Theatre Club, as censors determined it could
not be performed in public. 'Once Eddie had been
squarely placed in his social context, among his people,'
Miller noted, 'the myth-like feeling of the story emerged of
itself ... Red Hook is full of Greek tragedies.'

1957   Cited for contempt of Congress for refusing to co-operate
with HUAC. On the steps of the United States Congress,
and with Monroe on his arm, he vows to appeal against
the conviction. Monroe buys all members of Congress a
year's subscription to *I.F. Stone's Weekly*. First television
production of *Death of a Salesman* (ITA, UK). *Arthur Miller's
Collected Plays* is published, and his short story, 'The
Misfits', appears in *Esquire Magazine*.

1958–   The US Court of Appeals overturns his conviction
59   for contempt of Congress. Elected to the National
Institute of Arts and Letters and receives the Gold Medal
for Drama.

1961   Miller and Monroe divorce (granted in Mexico on the
grounds of 'incompatibility'). *The Misfits*, a black-and-

white film directed by John Huston featuring the actress
in her first serious dramatic role, is released for wide
distribution. Miller calls his scenario 'an eastern western'
and bases the plot on his short story of the same name.
Co-stars include Clark Gable, Montgomery Clift, Eli
Wallach and Thelma Ritter. *The Crucible: An Opera in Four
Acts* by Robert Ward and Bernard Stambler is recorded.
Sidney Lumet directs a movie version of *A View from the
Bridge* with Raf Vallone and Carol Lawrence. Miller's
mother, Augusta, dies.

1962   Marries Austrian-born Inge Morath, a photographer with
Magnum, the agency founded in 1947 by Henri Cartier-
Bresson. Marilyn Monroe, aged thirty-six, dies. His
daughter, Rebecca Augusta, is born in September. NBC
broadcasts an adaptation of *Focus* with James Whitmore
and Colleen Dewhurst.

1963   Publishes a children's book, *Jane's Blanket*. Returns to Ann
Arbor to deliver annual Hopwood Awards lecture, 'On
Recognition'.

1964   Visits the Mauthausen death camp with Inge Morath and
covers the Nazi trials in Frankfurt, Germany, for the *New
York Herald Tribune*. Reconciles with Kazan. *Incident at Vichy*,
whose through-line is 'It's not your guilt I want, it's your
responsibility', opens in New York, as does *After the Fall*. The
former is the first of the playwright's works to be banned in
the Soviet Union. The latter Miller says 'is not about
Marilyn' and that she is 'hardly the play's *raison d'etre*'.

1965   Elected president of PEN, the international organisation
of writers dedicated to fighting all forms of censorship.
American premiere of the two-act version of *A View from
the Bridge* is performed Off-Broadway. Laurence Olivier's
production of *The Crucible*, starring Colin Blakely and
Joyce Redman, is staged in London at the Old Vic by the
National Theatre. Returns to Ann Arbor, where his
daughter Jane is now a student, to participate in the first
teach-in in the US concerning the Vietnam conflict.

1966   First sound recording of *A View from the Bridge*. In Rome
Marcello Mastroianni and Monica Vitti play the parts of
Quentin and Maggie in Franco Zeffirelli's Italian
production of *After the Fall*. Miller's father, Isidore, dies.

1967   *I Don't Need You Any More*, a collection of short stories, is
published. Sound recording of *Incident at Vichy*. Television

production of *The Crucible* is broadcast on CBS. Visits
Moscow and tries to persuade Soviet writers to join PEN.
Playwright-in-Residence at the University of Michigan.
His son, Daniel, is born in January.

1968　*The Price*, which the playwright called 'a quartet', 'the most
specific play I've ever written', opens on Broadway. Sound
recording of *After the Fall*. Attends the Democratic National
Convention in Chicago as a delegate from Roxbury,
Connecticut. Leads peace march against the war in South-
East Asia with the Reverend Sloan Coffin, Jr, at Yale
University in New Haven. *Death of a Salesman* sells its
millionth copy.

1969　*In Russia*, a collaborative project with text by Miller and
photography by Morath, is published. Visits Prague in a
show of support for Czech writers; meets Vaclav Havel.
Retires as president of PEN.

1970　Miller's works are banned in the Soviet Union, a result of
his efforts to free dissident writers. *Fame* and *The Reason
Why*, two one-act plays, are produced; the latter is filmed
at his home in Connecticut.

1971　Television productions of *A Memory of Two Mondays* on
PBS and *The Price* on NBC. Sound recording of *An Enemy
of the People*. *The Portable Arthur Miller* is published.

1972　*The Creation of the World and Other Business* opens at the
Schubert Theatre in New York on 30 November. Attends
the Democratic National Convention in Miami as a
delegate. First sound recording of *The Crucible*.

1973　PBS broadcasts Stacy Keach's television adaptation of
Incident at Vichy, with Harris Yulin as Leduc. Champions
the case of Peter Reilly, an eighteen-year-old falsely
convicted of manslaughter for his mother's murder; four
years later, all charges are dismissed. *After the Fall* with
Faye Dunaway is televised on NBC. Teaches mini-course
at the University of Michigan; students perform early
drafts of scenes from *The American Clock*.

1974　*Up from Paradise*, musical version of *The Creation of the World
and Other Business*, is staged at the Power Center for the
Performing Arts at the University of Michigan. With
music by Stanley Silverman and cover design by Al
Hirschfield, Miller calls it his 'heavenly cabaret'.

1977　A second collaborative project with Inge Morath, *In the
Country*, is published. Petitions the Czech government to

halt arrests of dissident writers. The *Archbishop's Ceiling* opens at the Kennedy Center in Washington, DC. Miller said he wanted to dramatise 'what happens … when people know they are … at all times talking to Power, whether through a bug or a friend who really is an informer'.

1978 *The Theater Essays of Arthur Miller* is published. NBC broadcasts the film of *Fame* starring Richard Benjamin. Belgian National Theatre mounts the twenty-fifth anniversary production of *The Crucible*; this time Miller can attend.

1979 *Chinese Encounters*, with Inge Morath, is published. Michael Rudman directs a major revival of *Death of a Salesman* at the National Theatre in London, with Warren Mitchell as Willy Loman.

1980 *Playing for Time*, the film based on Fania Fenelon's autobiography *The Musicians of Auschwitz*, is broadcast nationally on CBS, with Vanessa Redgrave and Jane Alexander. ('I tried to treat it as a story meaningful to the survivors, by which I mean all of us. I didn't want it to be a mere horror story.') *The American Clock* has its first performance at the Spoleto Festival in South Carolina, then opens in New York with the playwright's sister, Joan Copeland, as Rose Baum, a role based on their mother. Miller sees his play as 'a mural', 'a mosaic', 'a story of America talking to itself … There's never been a society that hasn't had a clock running on it, and you can't help wondering – How long?'

1981 Second volume of *Arthur Miller's Collected Plays* is published. Delivers keynote address on the fiftieth anniversary of the Hopwood Awards Program in Ann Arbor.

1982 Two one-act plays that represent 'the colors of memory', *Elegy for a Lady* and *Some Kind of Love Story*, are produced as a double-bill at the Long Wharf Theatre in Connecticut under the title *2 by A.M.*

1983 Directs *Death of a Salesman* at the People's Art Theatre in Beijing, part of a cultural exchange to mark the early stage of the opening of diplomatic relations between the United States and the People's Republic of China. Ying Ruocheng plays Willy Loman in his own Chinese translation. *I Think About You a Great Deal*, a monologue written as a tribute to Vaclav Havel, appears in *Cross Currents*, University of Michigan.

1984   *'Salesman' in Beijing* is published. The texts of *Elegy for a Lady* and *Some Kind of Love Story* are printed under a new title, *Two-Way Mirror*. Receives Kennedy Center Honors for lifetime achievement. Reworks the script of *The American Clock* for Peter Wood's London production at the National Theatre.

1985   Twenty-five million viewers see Dustin Hoffman play Willy Loman, with John Malkovich as Biff and Kate Reid as Linda in the production of *Death of a Salesman* shown on CBS. Goes to Turkey with Harold Pinter for PEN as an ambassador for freedom of speech. Serves as delegate at a meeting of Soviet and American writers in Vilnius, Lithuania, where he attacks Russian authorities for their continuing anti-Semitism and persecution of *samizdat* writers. *The Archbishop's Ceiling* is produced in the UK by the Bristol Old Vic. Completes adaptation of *Playing for Time* as a stage play.

1986   One of fifteen writers and scientists invited to meet Mikhail Gorbachev to discuss Soviet policies. The Royal Shakespeare Company uses a revised script of *The Archbishop's Ceiling* for its London production in the Barbican Pit.

1987   Miller publishes *Timebends: A Life*, his autobiography. Characterising it as 'a preemptive strike' against future chroniclers, he discusses his relationship with Marilyn Monroe in public for the first time. *Clara* and *I Can't Remember Anything* open as a double-bill at Lincoln Center in New York under the title *Danger: Memory!* Broadcasts of *The Golden Years* on BBC Radio and Jack O'Brien's television production of *All My Sons* on PBS. Michael Gambon stars as Eddie Carbone in Alan Ayckbourn's intimate production of *A View from the Bridge* at the National Theatre in London. University of East Anglia names its site for American Studies the Arthur Miller Centre.

1988   Publishes 'Waiting for the Teacher', a nineteen-stanza free-verse poem, in *Ha'aretz*, the Tel Aviv-based liberal newspaper, on the occasion of the fiftieth anniversary of the founding of the State of Israel.

1990   *Everybody Wins*, directed by Karel Reisz with Debra

Winger and Nick Nolte, is released: 'Through the evolution of the story – a murder that took place before the story opens – we will be put through an exercise in experiencing reality and unreality.' Television production of *An Enemy of the People* on PBS. Josette Simon plays Maggie as a sultry jazz singer in Michael Blakemore's London revival of *After the Fall* at the National Theatre, where *The Crucible* also joins the season's repertory in Howard Davies's production starring Zoë Wannamaker and Tom Wilkinson. Updated version of *The Man Who Had All the Luck* is staged by Paul Unwin in a joint production by the Bristol Old Vic and the Young Vic in London.

1991   *The Last Yankee* premieres as a one-act play. *The Ride Down Mount Morgan*, 'a moral farce', has its world premiere in London: 'The play is really a kind of nightmare.' Television adaptation of *Clara* on the Arts & Entertainment Network. Receives Mellon Bank Award for lifetime achievement in the humanities.

1992   *Homely Girl, A Life* is published with artwork by Louise Bourgeois in a Peter Blum edition. Writes satirical op-ed piece for the *New York Times* urging an end to capital punishment in the US.

1993   Expanded version of *The Last Yankee* opens at the Manhattan Theatre Club in New York. Television version of *The American Clock* on TNT with the playwright's daughter, Rebecca, in the role of Edie.

1994   *Broken Glass*, a work 'full of ambiguities' that takes 'us back to the time when the social contract was being torn up', has a pre-Broadway run at the Long Wharf Theatre in Connecticut; opens at the Booth Theatre in New York on 24 April. David Thacker's London production wins the Olivier Award for Best Play.

1995   Tributes to the playwright on the occasion of his eightieth birthday are held in England and the US. Receives William Inge Festival Award for Distinguished Achievement in American Theater. *Homely Girl, A Life and Other Stories*, is published. In England the collection appears under the title *Plain Girl*. Darryl V. Jones directs a production of *A View from the Bridge* in Washington, DC, and resets the play in a community of Domincan immigrants. The Arthur Miller Society is founded by Steve Centola.

1996   Revised and expanded edition of *The Theater Essays of Arthur Miller* is published. Receives the Edward Albee Last Frontier Playwright Award. Rebecca Miller and Daniel Day-Lewis are married.

1997   *The Crucible*, produced by the playwright's son, Robert A. Miller, is released for wide distribution and is nominated for an Academy Award. Revised version of *The Ride Down Mount Morgan* performed at the Williamstown Playhouse in Massachusetts. BBC airs television version of *Broken Glass*, with Margot Leicester and Henry Goodman repeating their roles from the award-winning London production.

1998   *Mr Peters' Connections* opens in New York with Peter Falk. Revival of *A View from the Bridge* by the Roundabout Theatre Company wins two Tony Awards. Revised version of *The Ride Down Mount Morgan* on Broadway. Miller is named Distinguished Inaugural Senior Fellow of the American Academy in Berlin.

1999   Robert Falls's fiftieth anniversary production of *Death of a Salesman*, featuring Brian Dennehy as Willy Loman, moves from the Goodman Theater in Chicago and opens on Broadway, where it wins the Tony Award for Best Revival of a Play. Co-authors the libretto with Arnold Weinstein for William Bolcom's opera of *A View from the Bridge*, which has its world premiere at the Lyric Opera of Chicago.

2000   Patrick Stewart reprises his role as Lyman Felt in *The Ride Down Mount Morgan* on Broadway, where *The Price* is also revived (with Harris Yulin). Major eighty-fifth birthday celebrations are organised by Christopher Bigsby at the University of East Anglia and by Enoch Brater at the University of Michigan, where plans are announced to build a new theatre named in his honour; it opens officially on 29 March 2007 ('whoever thought when I was saving $500 to come to the University of Michigan that it would come to this'). 'Up to a certain point the human being is completely unpredictable. That's what keeps me going … You live long enough, you don't rust.' *Echoes Down the Corridor*, a collection of essays from 1944 to 2000, is published. Miller and Morath travel to Cuba with William and Rose Styron and meet Fidel Castro and the Colombian writer Gabriel García Márquez.

2001   Williamstown Theater Festival revives *The Man Who Had All the Luck*. Laura Dern and William H. Macy star in a xvi   A View from the Bridge

film based on the 1945 novel *Focus*. Miller is named the
Jefferson Lecturer in the Humanities by NEH and
receives the John H. Finley Award for Exemplary Service
to New York City. His speech *On Politics and the Art of
Acting* is published.

2002　Revivals in New York of *The Man Who Had All the Luck*
and *The Crucible*, the latter with Liam Neeson as John
Proctor. *Resurrection Blues* has its world premiere at the
Guthrie Theatre in Minneapolis. Miller receives a major
international award in Spain, the Premio Principe de
Asturias de las Letras. Death of Inge Morath.

2003　Awarded the Jerusalem Prize. His brother, Kermit Miller,
dies on 17 October. *The Price* is performed at the Tricycle
Theatre in London.

2004　*Finishing the Picture* opens at the Goodman Theatre in
Chicago. *After the Fall* revived in New York. Appears on a
panel at the University of Michigan with Mark Lamos,
who directs students in scenes from Miller's rarely
performed plays.

2005　Miller dies of heart failure in his Connecticut home on 10
February. Public memorial service is held on 9 May at the
Majestic Theatre in New York, with 1,500 in attendance.
Asked what he wanted to be remembered for, the
playwright said, 'A few good parts for actors.'

Plot

Act One

The play begins with the narrator, the lawyer Alfieri, directly addressing the audience from his office. His speeches punctuate many of the scenes, and he is also a participant in the action. Alfieri's opening speech directly relates the events that will unfold during the play, set in Brooklyn, to the attitudes of the Italian-Americans and their forebears in Sicily. As narrator, he tells how they consider meeting a priest or a lawyer 'unlucky', associating these figures with impending disasters. He thinks that this attitude lies in 'three thousand years of distrust'. He proclaims that: 'Justice is very important here.' Finally, he explains that in his legal practice he deals mostly with longshoremen and their wives, fathers and grandfathers in compensation cases, evictions and petty squabbles. Yet every few years a case comes along that is different from the petty troubles of these poor people, and as he listens to it, he surmises that some lawyer thousands of years ago heard the same complaint, 'powerless as I, and watched it run its bloody course'. He concludes with 'This one's name was Eddie Carbone, a longshoreman . . .'.

The first scene takes place in the Red Hook apartment of Eddie Carbone and his wife, Beatrice, who have raised her niece, Catherine, since she was a child. Catherine is seventeen and on the verge of becoming a woman. Eddie has just come home from work and Catherine greets him excitedly. He notices that she is 'dressed up', in a new skirt and with a different hairdo, and he wants to know where she is going. Catherine has some news for him, but wants to wait for Beatrice to come into the room. Eddie thinks Catherine's skirt is too short and expresses concern that she gives him the 'willies' when she walks 'wavy' down the street. Moreover, he does not like the looks that men give her at the candy store and when she wears her new high heels. Eddie's criticism almost brings Catherine to tears; he explains that he promised Catherine's mother on her deathbed that he would be responsible for her. He calls her a 'baby', and admonishes her for waving at a neighbour called Louis out of the apartment window. He tells Catherine that she is getting to be a 'big girl' and cannot be so friendly with men.

He then asks Catherine to call Beatrice from the kitchen because he has news that her cousins – illegal immigrants also known as 'submarines' – have landed in New York harbour. The two men will be staying with the Carbones. Beatrice is overjoyed at their impending arrival; but not expecting them so soon, she worries about feeding them and about the condition of the apartment. Eddie assures her that the men will think they are in a millionaire's house compared to their circumstances in Italy. Eddie teases Beatrice about her generosity. Beatrice is concerned that Eddie will be angry with her if the living situation turns unpleasant, but Eddie cautions that if they all keep quiet about the presence of the illegal relatives, nothing can happen.

Catherine returns to the exciting news that she wanted to tell Eddie at the beginning of the scene. The principal of her school has arranged for her to get a job as a stenographer at a plumbing company. Eddie is reluctant to let her accept because he wants her to finish her secretarial school training. But Catherine explains that the principal advises that she should take the job, and that he will allow her to sit the examination for a certificate at the end of the year because she is the best student in the class. Eddie is still uneasy. He does not like the neighbourhood near the Brooklyn Navy Yard where the company is located and where she will be exposed to unsavoury men like plumbers and sailors. Beatrice explains to Eddie that Catherine is not a baby any longer, saying: 'She's seventeen years old, you gonna keep her in the house all her life?' When Catherine returns to the room, Eddie looks at her with tears in his eyes and tells her she looks 'like a madonna'. He agrees to allow her to work, but warns her: 'Don't trust nobody.'

Their conversation then returns to the imminent arrival of Beatrice's cousins. Eddie reiterates to Catherine and Beatrice the importance of not speaking about their status as illegal immigrants. He tells them: 'You don't see nothin' and you don't know nothin'.' He warns them that there are 'stool pigeons' all over the neighbourhood who would inform the Immigration Bureau. Eddie and Beatrice both recall an incident that occurred in the neighbourhood years ago. A family had an uncle whom they were hiding in their house and their fourteen-year-old son snitched to Immigration. The boy was punished by his father and five brothers who dragged him down the stairs in their house and spat on him in the street in front of the entire neighbourhood. When Catherine asks what happened to him, Eddie says, 'You'll never see him no more, a guy do a thing like that? How's he gonna show his face?'

Their conversation again returns to Catherine's job when Eddie says, 'So you gonna start Monday, heh, Madonna?' and he is moved to tears as he expresses that he never thought she 'would ever grow up'. When Catherine leaves to get Eddie his cigar, Beatrice and Eddie are alone for a minute and Eddie asks Beatrice if she is 'mad' at him; Beatrice retorts with, 'You're the one is mad.' The scene ends and the lights come up on Alfieri, who describes Eddie as 'a good man as he had to be in a life that was hard and even'; then he announces the arrival of the cousins.

When the two cousins arrive, Catherine is struck by the physical differences between the two brothers. The older, married man, Marco, is dark-complexioned while the younger, unmarried man is light with blond hair. Beatrice and Eddie are interested in the living and working conditions in post-war Sicily, and the men explain the occasional construction and field work they do. Marco is particularly interested in working regularly on the docks so he can send money back to his wife, who will then be able to feed the three children better and buy medicine for the eldest child, who is ill. He eventually wants to return home. Catherine focuses her attention on Rodolpho who, in contrast to his brother, wants to become an American and

stay forever. Rodolpho has an exuberant spirit and dreams
about returning to Italy as a rich man with a motorcycle.
Rodolpho reveals that he is also a singer who took the place
of a sick baritone one night and sang to great acclaim in the
garden of a local hotel. Marco affectionately mocks the
youthful bravado of his brother, but Catherine is enthralled
and coaxes Rodolpho to perform his version of the song
'Paper Doll'. Eddie is not happy about the performance and
warns that his singing might attract unwanted attention to
the illegal submarines. Then he turns to criticise Catherine
for wearing high heels, and the scene ends with Eddie sizing
up Rodolpho, whom he regards suspiciously.

The next scene begins with brief commentary by the
narrator Alfieri, who tells the audience that 'Eddie never
expected to have a destiny'. A couple of weeks have passed
and trouble has come to the Carbones. The first part of the
scene takes place in front of the Carbone apartment where
Eddie is standing at the doorway. Beatrice comes along and
Eddie is worried because it is after eight o'clock and
Catherine and Rodolpho are not yet home from the
movies. Although he seems to be concerned about
Rodolpho being picked up by the immigration authorities,
actually Eddie does not like the romantic relationship that
has grown between Catherine and Rodolpho. He transfers
his jealousy into an assault on Rodolpho's masculinity. He
tells Beatrice that Rodolpho gives him the 'heebie-jeebies',
explaining that he is not the kind of man who should be
Catherine's husband. He does not like the fact that
Rodolpho sings on the ships, that his blond hair makes him
look like a chorus girl, and that other longshoreman call
him 'Paper Doll' and 'Canary'. When Eddie expresses
frustration that Beatrice apparently does not understand
the problem, she explains that she has 'other worries' and
asks Eddie when she is 'gonna be a wife again'. Beatrice
and Eddie have not slept together in almost three months;
Eddie refuses to discuss the issue further, claiming he is
worried that Rodolpho is taking Catherine 'for a ride'.
Beatrice retreats into the house and Eddie encounters three
neighbourhood longshoremen on the street who talk about

how Marco works like a bull when off-loading ships and
Rodolpho's sense of humour.

When Catherine and Rodolpho return home from their
date, Eddie's anger, especially with Rodolpho, is apparent.
He dismisses Rodolpho so he can talk to Catherine alone.
Catherine attempts to explain to Eddie that Rodolpho
'blesses' him, but Eddie counters that Rodolpho does not
respect Catherine because, if she were not an orphan,
Rodolpho would have to ask the permission of her father to
date her. When Catherine explains to Eddie the proper
respect which Rodolpho exhibits, Eddie proclaims that
Rodolpho is just 'bowin'' to his passport', i.e. merely using the
ploy of marriage to obtain American citizenship. They take
their argument into the apartment where Eddie asks Beatrice
to 'straighten' Catherine out, and then he storms out of the
apartment. Beatrice explains to Catherine that Eddie would
not be satisfied with any beau of Catherine's and that she
cannot be taking orders from him any more because she is
no longer a girl now but a woman. Beatrice tells her that, 'If
you act like a baby, he'll treat you like a baby.' Beatrice
displays both awareness and sensitivity to the relationship
between Eddie and Catherine. She tells her niece that she
should not walk around the apartment in her slip, or sit and
watch Eddie shave while he is in his underwear. Beatrice says
that she has previously tried to tell her about this
inappropriate behaviour, but Catherine now has to realise
that she is a grown woman and Eddie is a man.

The next scene begins with brief commentary by Alfieri
about a 'passion' which he perceived had moved into
Eddie's body. Eddie has come to Alfieri's law office to seek
advice about finding legal recourse to stop Catherine's
relationship with Rodolpho. Alfieri explains that there is
nothing illegal about a girl falling in love with an immigrant,
but Eddie's frustration over Rodolpho's spending habits, his
masculinity, his high singing voice and his sewing ability is
evident. He says, 'The guy ain't right.' When Alfieri
explains that the only legal question is the manner in which
Marco and Rodolpho entered the country, Eddie explains
that he wouldn't do anything about that. Alfieri gently tries

to explain to Eddie that sometimes there is 'too much love' from a father to a daughter or niece – as Alfieri and the audience clearly understand is so in Eddie's case. Eddie does not completely understand and continues to object to Rodolpho's stealing Catherine from him. Even when Alfieri is more candid, saying, 'She can't marry you, can she?' Eddie says, 'What the hell you talkin' about, marry me?' After Eddie leaves the office, Alfieri again addresses the audience, explaining that after that meeting with Eddie, he realised the situation would end badly and that he was powerless to prevent it.

The final scene of Act One takes place in the Carbone apartment one evening a short time later. Beatrice and Catherine are clearing the dinner table and Eddie, Marco and Rodolpho are in the living room. Catherine initiates conversation about Marco and Rodolpho's life in Italy, fishing and sailing. Eddie is in a particularly surly and contradictory mood. When Beatrice enquires of Marco whether his wife is receiving the money he is sending, Eddie takes the opportunity to ask if there are any 'surprise' children when the fathers eventually return home. After Marco explains that the women wait, Rodolpho adds that their town is 'more strict'. Eddie uses this as an opening to tell Rodopho that the States are not so free – an obvious objection to Rodolpho's freedom with Catherine and his risking arrest by Immigration. Marco attempts to alleviate Eddie's concerns. After an awkward silence, Catherine asks Rodolpho to dance to a new record they have bought – 'Paper Doll', the same song that Rodolpho sang on the night of his arrival. While Rodolpho and Catherine dance, Beatrice, Eddie and Marco talk about how Rodolpho cooks for the crew on the fishing excursions the men take. To Eddie this is another example – along with the singing and sewing – of Rodolpho's lack of masculinity. During this scene, Eddie has been twisting his newspaper in frustration as Catherine and Rodolpho continue dancing. Eddie then suggests that Rodolpho and Marco should go to the fights next Saturday night. When the men agree, Eddie offers to teach Rodolpho how to box. He proceeds to show him a few punches, ultimately landing a blow that staggers Rodolpho. After this obvious and planned humiliation, Rodolpho initiates the resumption of dancing with Catherine. The previously polite and deferential Marco, now challenges Eddie to pick up a chair by one leg. Eddie attempts this, but is unable to perform the task. Marco then kneels, grasps the leg, picks up the chair and lifts it high, facing Eddie with the chair raised menacingly over his head.

Act Two

The second act begins with a brief set-up by Alfieri: it is 23 December, a case of Scotch whisky had 'slipped' while being unloaded on the docks, Beatrice is shopping, Marco is working. Rodolpho had not been hired that day; consequently, he and Catherine are alone in the Carbone apartment.

Clearly upset about the conflict that their relationship is causing and perhaps aroused by Eddie's accusation, Catherine asks Rodolpho if he would consider living in Italy after they marry. Rodolpho absolutely refuses to consider this, explaining to Catherine that there is nothing in Italy for them to go to: 'How can I bring you from a rich country to suffer in a poor country?' He is adamant; he knows that Eddie has raised these doubts in Catherine, and he is insulted. Catherine explains her complicated feelings for Eddie: she feels indebted to him for his goodness in having raised her and she is torn about rejecting him. She reveals considerable awareness of Eddie's needs as a man and husband. But Rodolpho's and Catherine's love is genuine, and Rodolpho convinces her that she must grow and, like a little bird, fly away. They retreat into the bedroom.

At that moment Eddie comes home drunk. When he calls for Beatrice in the apartment, Catherine, followed by Rodolpho, emerges from the bedroom. Eddie is furious and tells Rodolpho to pack his things and leave. When Catherine proclaims her intention to leave as well, Eddie tells her that she is going nowhere. But Catherine proclaims, 'I'm not gonna be a baby any more!' Eddie suddenly

reaches out to her and kisses her on the mouth. When
Rodolpho tries to stop him, Eddie in turn attacks, pinning
Rodolpho's arms, laughing and suddenly kissing Rodolpho,
humiliating him. Eddie then orders Rodolpho to leave the
apartment, threatening to kill him if he ever lays a hand on
Catherine again.

The next scene begins with Alfieri's narration about
another visit by Eddie to his office a few days after the
confrontation in the apartment. Alfieri recalls the fixed look
in Eddie's eyes, which he compares to tunnels. Eddie tells
Alfieri that Beatrice will be moving Marco and Rodolpho to
a room in an upstairs apartment. In discussing Eddie's
attack on Rodolpho, Alfieri judges that Rodolpho was just
not strong enough to break Eddie's grip on him. However,
Eddie insists that Rodolpho did not fight back because the
'guy ain't right'. When Alflieri asks Eddie why he humiliated
Rodolpho, Eddie claims that he wanted Catherine to see
what Rodolpho really is. But Eddie again asks Alfieri what
legal recourse he has to stop the marriage that is soon to
take place between his wife's niece and the 'submarine'.
Alfieri explains to Eddie that morally and legally he has no
rights whatsoever. Alfieri warns him further that the law is
nature and 'a river will drown him if he tries to buck it'.
Eddie leaves in dismay.

The lights come up on Eddie at a public telephone,
making a call to the Immigration Bureau. He reports illegal
immigrants living at his address, the same heinous act he
scorned earlier in the play.

The next scene is in the Carbone apartment, where
Beatrice is taking down Christmas decorations. Eddie enters
and discovers that Marco and Rodolpho have already
moved to an upstairs apartment. Eddie and Beatrice argue.
She regrets that she ever agreed to have her cousins to stay
in their apartment, but she wants to know why he
humiliated Rodolpho in front of Catherine. Now that they
are gone, Eddie asserts command of his home and demands
his 'respect' back from Beatrice, especially about references
to their sex life. Beatrice tells him that Rodolpho and
Catherine plan to marry the next week because her niece is

concerned about him getting picked up by the immigration
authorities; if they marry, he can begin the process of
applying for citizenship. Beatrice tells Eddie that despite
what has occurred, Catherine would still like his blessing at
the wedding.

Catherine comes down from the apartment upstairs as
Beatrice attempts a reconciliation between them. However,
Eddie is resolute and tries to convince Catherine not to
marry; she is equally determined to go ahead with her plans.
When Catherine asks Beatrice's permission to take a few
pillowcases upstairs, Eddie discovers that there are
additional illegal boarders in the apartment where
Rodolpho and Marco are now lodged. Eddie panics and,
without revealing that he has informed, demands that
Catherine move Rodolpho and Marco out of the apartment
on the grounds that mixing with other illegals will attract
attention. At that moment the immigration officers arrive
and both Beatrice and Catherine realise what Eddie has
done. As the group of submarines is arrested and brought
out on the street in front of the apartment house, Marco
lunges for Eddie, accusing him of betraying him and his
brother to the authorities. The crowd of neighbours gather
one by one and shun Eddie, who screams that Marco is
'gonna take that back'.

The next scene is set in the reception room of a prison
where Alfieri serves as legal counsel to Marco and
Rodolpho. He will be able to bail out Marco if he promises
not to take revenge on Eddie. Alfieri explains that Marco
will be deported in any case, but that Rodolpho, because he
is going to marry Catherine, can become an American
citizen. Marco and Alfieri discuss what 'honorable' action is.
Marco explains that in his country Eddie would already be
dead for his action; and Alfieri explains that to promise not
to kill is not dishonourable. Marco wants to know where the
law is that governs the despicable degradation which Eddie
has brought upon Marco's blood and kin. Alfieri counters
with, 'Only God makes justice.'

The final scene takes place in the Carbone apartment the
afternoon of Catherine and Rodolpho's wedding. Beatrice is

dressed to leave for the nuptials and Eddie tells her not to
come back home if she goes. Eddie still wants his 'respect'
back and demands that Marco apologise to him before any
wedding takes place. Catherine yells at Eddie calling him a
rat who belongs in the sewer; Eddie moves to attack her, but
Beatrice intervenes, then decides not to attend the wedding.
At that moment Rodolpho rushes into the apartment
warning that Marco is coming to avenge himself on Eddie.
Rodolpho wants Eddie to avoid this confrontation and
attempts a reconciliation by kissing his hand and
apologising. Eddie rejects his overture because he wants
nothing but Marco to give him back his 'name', which he
has besmirched in the neighbourhood. Beatrice says to
Eddie: 'You want somethin' else, Eddie and you can never
have her', finally stating the truth of what has been obvious
all along to everyone but Eddie. Eddie is horrified, but at
that moment Marco arrives in the street in front of the
apartment and calls out Eddie's name. The whole
neighbourhood has gathered to witness this final
confrontation. Eddie goes out to the street, where Marco
calls him an animal as he strikes him and demands that
Eddie get down on his knees before him. Eddie pulls a knife
on Marco, but in the ensuing struggle, Marco turns the knife
on Eddie, mortally wounding him.

The play ends with final commentary by Alfieri, who
acknowledges how wrong Eddie was and that his death was
useless but inevitable. Nevertheless, he mourns him with 'a
certain alarm', searching for the meaning that might be
found in the tragedy of his death.

Commentary

Literary, historical and social context

A View from the Bridge ended a remarkably productive time in Arthur Miller's career when he stood, along with Tennessee Williams, as one of America's most distinguished playwrights. The plays he wrote during this period – *All My Sons* (1947), *Death of Salesman* (1949), *An Enemy of the People* (1950), *The Crucible* (1953), *A View from the Bridge* (one act, 1955) and *A View from the Bridge* (two acts, 1956) – are dramas upon which his lasting critical reputation will undoubtedly be judged. After the London production of *View from the Bridge* in 1956, Miller did not have another original play produced on either the New York or London stages until *After the Fall* in 1964. Miller first wrote *A View from the Bridge* as a one-act play with a companion piece, *A Memory of Two Mondays*, which premiered in New York in 1955. Miller wrote the two-act version in 1956, which premiered in London. Miller considered the two-act play the definitive version, including it in the first edition of his *Collected Plays* in 1957.

A View from the Bridge had a long period of gestation. In 1947, after his success with *All My Sons*, Miller became intrigued with writing about the Italian immigrant society of the Brooklyn docks. He had noticed graffiti during his walks across the Brooklyn Bridge that read: 'Dovè Pete Panto?' which translates from the Italian as: 'Where is Pete Panto?' The message also began appearing on subway stations and on office buildings at the Court Street Civic Center in downtown Brooklyn. Miller learned from newspaper coverage that Pete Panto was a young longshoreman who had challenged the powerful Mafia leadership of the seamen's union and had mysteriously disappeared, effectively ending the threat of an investigation of the union's corruption. Miller was fascinated by the idea of writing about the tragic end of this heroic man. He began researching the criminal underworld of the Brooklyn docksides by visiting the piers and attempting to find out the truth behind Panto's fate. However, Miller was stymied by the intimidated silence of the longshoremen, who feared speaking out against their bosses and the hiring traditions transported from their native Sicily.

Nearly deciding to give up his project, Miller unexpectedly received a phone call from Mitch Berenson, a union organiser, and Vinny Longhi, a lawyer, who were attempting to continue Pete Panto's resistance to the longshoremen union's power structure. After Miller offered to write about their plight, they gave him the opportunity to enter the mysterious underbelly of this corrupt world. He learned about the lives and culture of the longshoremen, many of whom he befriended, often visiting their homes in their Red Hook neighbourhood. In 1947 to 1948 Miller even accompanied Longhi on a trip to Sicily where he hoped to solicit support for his cause in an upcoming union election. In Italy Miller absorbed Sicilian society and came to understand the cultural connection between the American immigrants and their native land.

During this time, Longhi told Miller the story of another longshoreman who had informed the Immigration Bureau about two brothers who were related to him and living illegally in his house. In order to break up the relationship between his niece and one of the cousins, the longshoreman had informed the immigration authorities, an action which made him a pariah in his neighbourhood. Local gossip said that he was killed by one of the brothers. In an essay, 'On Social Plays', which Miller wrote as an introduction to the published one-act play, Miller explained that when he first heard the tale in his Brooklyn neighbourhood, he thought he had heard it before as 'some re-enactment of a Greek myth'. To Miller, it seemed the two illegal immigrants set out from Italy as if it were two thousand years ago; he was awed by the destiny of the immigrants and their informer, as though this was almost the work of Fate. Miller fiddled with a screenplay about the story, but then, not quite ready to dramatise the tale fully, dropped it after his trip to Sicily and eventually became consumed with writing *Death of a Salesman* in 1948 and with the production of that masterpiece in 1949.

During the run of *Salesman*, Miller wrote a screenplay, *The Hook*, about his experience on the docks, focusing on Pete Panto's doomed attempt to overthrow the Mafia gangsters who ruled the New York waterfront. After he read the script, Elia Kazan, the renowned film and stage director of *All My Sons* and *Death of a Salesman*, thought the film was a viable project for him to direct. Consequently, in 1951 Miller and Kazan took a trip to Hollywood to obtain the backing from a major studio. The negotiations for the film broke down when the Hollywood producers were reluctant to make a film critical of the unions and demanded unrealistic changes such as depicting the union crooks as communists, which Miller refused to do. The studios also performed background checks on Miller and Kazan – an indication of the coming hysteria about communism just beginning. In Hollywood, Miller also met the starlet Marilyn Monroe for the first time.

After his trip, disappointed at the commercial failure of his rewrite of Henrik Ibsen's *An Enemy of the People* (1950), Miller returned to the tale of the Italian longshoreman who had snitched on his relatives, working on the play for several months under the title 'An Italian Tragedy', before abandoning it again. It was not until 1954 that Miller would complete the play.

After his frustration with the critical reception of *The Crucible* in 1953, his controversial play about the Salem Witch Trials, Miller received a phone call from the actor Martin Ritt, who asked him to write a one-act play for a group of actors who had a theatre available for use on Sunday evenings and wanted to act in a play without any commercial restraints. Miller agreed and wrote his one-act *A Memory of Two Mondays*, which is based on his own life – the dramatised recollection of the summer he spent working as a clerk in an auto-parts factory in Manhattan before he attended the University of Michigan. Ritt loved the play, and asked Miller if he had another one-act play to begin the evening, a so-called 'curtain raiser'. Thus, Miller returned to 'An Italian Tragedy' which suddenly 'seemed to fall into place as a one-act with a single rising line of intensity leading inevitably to an explosive climax' (*Timebends*, 353). Miller realised that his difficulty in dramatising the story of the longshoreman was that he had worried too much over making it a full-length play for the Broadway theatre. He transformed 'An Italian Tragedy' into the drama of Eddie Carbone and his niece Catherine, writing the one-act version of what he now called *A View from the Bridge* in ten days. The title refers to the famous Brooklyn Bridge which spans the East River between Manhattan and Brooklyn at the foot of Brooklyn Heights, and not far from the Red Hook neighbourhood. However, when the original theatre for the Sunday performances was no longer available, Kermit Bloomgarden, the producer of *Death of a Salesman*, became enthusiastic about both one-act plays being performed by the same cast, and he offered a fully fledged Broadway production.

Miller originally wanted to dramatise the story of the informer without embellishment, exactly in 'its exposed skeleton' because he did not want to interfere with the 'myth-like march of the tale' toward its tragic ending. At this stage in his career, Miller was interested in writing modern American tragedies. For example, a few weeks after the production of *Death of a Salesman* opened, Miller wrote an op-ed piece for the *New York Times* entitled 'Tragedy and the Common Man', in which he made the case for Willy Loman as a modern tragic hero. Miller maintained that modern literature does not require characters to be royalty or leaders, as in the tragedies of other eras, and therefore fall from some great height. Rather he insisted: 'I think that the tragic feeling is evoked when we are in the presence of a character who is ready to lay down his life, if need be, to secure one thing – his sense of personal dignity. From Orestes to Hamlet, Medea to Macbeth, the underlying struggle is that of the individual attempting to gain his "rightful" position in his society.' Thus, Miller argues that a lowly man like Willy Loman could be considered a tragic hero. He clearly set his dramatic sights on achieving this in *A View from the Bridge*. Of course, the original attraction to him of Pete Panto's story was that he seemed a modern hero whose demise was a tragedy. Miller had also explored this notion in *The Crucible* with his hero John Proctor, and he aimed at a similar depiction for Eddie Carbone.

At this time in 1955, Miller was also clearly interested in exploring further the themes of betrayal, informing and adultery, which he had illustrated in *The Crucible*. For by the time he was writing the one-act version of *A View from the Bridge*, he had embarked on his affair with Marilyn Monroe, was about to divorce his wife, and was becoming a target of the House Un-American Activities Committee (HUAC). In 1950 the United States had begun a period of political and social upheaval that would have a lasting effect on Miller's career and personal life. During this time, Miller witnessed the rise of the Army/McCarthy hearings, conducted by the Wisconsin Senator, Joseph McCarthy, and the establishment of HUAC, which was revived after the Second World War in response to the 'Red Scare' from the Soviet Union and the fall of China to a Communist government. Citizens were called before the committee in order to admit to radical pasts, and its targets were often high-profile celebrities, especially in the entertainment world, whose appearance would guarantee major publicity for the committee. Miller and Kazan had discovered this in Hollywood with their attempt to get *The Hook* made, but during his writing of *The Crucible* and *A View from the Bridge* Miller would see his friends and colleagues – and eventually himself – targeted.

In fact, in April 1952 Miller decided to write *The Crucible* because he saw a 'living connection between myself and Salem, and between Salem and Washington'. Miller had planned an exploratory trip to Salem to research the original court records. Coincidentally, the day before he was to leave for Massachusetts he received a phone call from Elia Kazan who had been subpoenaed by HUAC. Kazan and Miller met in Connecticut where Kazan told Miller that he had decided to cooperate and testify about the names of other celebrities he had encountered at Communist Party meetings years earlier. Kazan's decision would cause a breach in his personal and professional relationship with Miller that would last until the next decade, when, in 1964, Kazan directed *After the Fall*. When Miller left Salem, he heard on his car radio a news report of Kazan's testimony before HUAC: he had 'named names'. In the next few months, the playwright Clifford Odets, whose work had had a major influence on Miller, would be called before the committee; he too named names. Lee J. Cobb, the original Willy Loman, was called, and he too succumbed to the power of the committee. Miller was struck by the political forces which cause men to inform on others. This became a central focus in *The Crucible* and one which he also carried over into *A View from the Bridge*.

Miller wanted *A View from the Bridge* to follow very closely the tale Vinny Longhi had told him, trying not to change its original shape. He hoped the audience would feel as he felt when he heard it for the first time – not with sympathy but with wonder. Miller admits that the meaning of Eddie's fate remained a mystery to him during and after writing the one-act play. But he was dissatisfied with the final result. The reviews were mixed and the production consequently had a disappointing run, closing after 149 performances, though Miller won his third Drama Critics' Circle Award. In *Timebends* he acknowledges that personal and professional distractions in his life caused him not to focus fully on writing the play as the Broadway hit which Bloomgarden wanted. Miller was deeply involved in his relationship with Marilyn Monroe at this time and was contemplating the painful divorce from his wife. Moreover, he continued to be distracted by personal attacks on him brought by his political views. In 1954, the American government refused to grant Miller a passport and visa for the European premiere of *The Crucible*, and his break with Kazan over his testimony received wide press coverage. In addition, while casting and rehearsing the one-act *A View from the Bridge*, Miller had been researching and writing a screenplay for the

New York Youth Board about juvenile delinquents. An investigator from HUAC warned the city administration about being associated with Miller because of his political opinions. In turn, the American Legion and the Catholic War Veterans applied pressure to stop the film because of Miller's 'Communist ties'. The project was stopped.

Miller had the opportunity to revise the play in 1956, a tumultuous year for him: committed to Monroe, he spent six weeks in April in Nevada to establish residency for a 'quickie' divorce. After filing for divorce, Miller had his celebrated hearing before HUAC. Following this, he and Monroe were married in late June, then the famous couple flew to England where Monroe was to star with Laurence Olivier in *The Prince and the Showgirl*, and where Miller revised the play into a two-act for the London production directed by Peter Brook.

The seemingly unlikely marriage between Miller and Monroe caused a media sensation, with headlines like 'Pinko Playwright Weds Sex Goddess'. Miller perceived that his relationship with Monroe would bring needed attention to the HUAC, whose influence had been waning. In May 1956, Miller was subpoenaed, and the hypocrisy of the committee was evident to him when his lawyer told him that the Pennsylvania Representative Francis E. Walter, chairman of the committee, proposed that the hearing could be cancelled if Monroe agreed to be photographed shaking hands with him. In Miller's testimony, he answered cordially the committee's questions about his association with political groups, and gave his opinions on freedom of speech, communist conspiracies, and figures like Elia Kazan and the poet Ezra Pound. At the end of his testimony, Miller was asked about his attendance at a meeting of communist writers a decade earlier. Miller freely admitted his presence, but refused to give the names of others in attendance. The committee already knew the names of attendees; they were concerned with Miller's compliance to their power and his betrayal of friends and colleagues. Miller was warned that he would be in contempt of Congress for refusing to answer, since he had chosen not to

claim the Fifth Amendment's constitutional protection
against self-incrimination. Miller still refused and, therefore,
was cited. Eventually he was tried for contempt of Congress
and was found guilty on two counts. His sentencing was
deferred for an appeal and in 1958 the US Court of Appeals
overturned his conviction.

In revising *A View from the Bridge* for the London
production, Miller responded to criticism of the sketchiness
of the characters in the one-act play. He enlarged the
psychological motivations of the principal characters –
Eddie Carbone, his wife Beatrice and their niece Catherine
– in order to emphasise the social consequences of the play's
central action: Eddie's desire for Catherine. The London
production received rave reviews and ran for 220
performances; a subsequent production in Paris ran for two
years.

Structure

In addition to the 1955 one-act version of *A View from the
Bridge* and the 1956 two-act version which premiered in
London, there is also a third version: Miller rewrote the end
for the 1957 Paris production because he was advised that a
French audience would not accept that Eddie and
Catherine could be unaware of the emotions between them.
Ostracised by his society, Eddie kills himself.

In the writing and production of the first version of *A View
from the Bridge*, Miller decided on the one-act form to 'recreate
my own feeling toward this tale – namely wonderment. It is
not designed primarily to draw tears or laughter from an
audience, but to strike a particular note of astonishment at
the way in which, and the reasons for which, a man will
endanger and risk and lose his very life' ('On Social Plays',
68). Miller explained that, 'Nothing was permitted which did
not advance the progress of Eddie's catastrophe in a most
direct way . . . [I felt] that I ought to deliver it onto the stage
as fact; that interpretation was inherent in the very existence
of the tale in the first place' (*A View from the Bridge*,

Introduction). Thus, the one-act version consists of ten scenes, performed without a break or intermission. Although the play is practically full-length in its running time, when writing it Miller said he 'did not know how to pull a curtain down anywhere before its end . . . I kept looking for an act curtain, a point of pause, but none ever developed' ('On Social Plays', 65). The New York production used sparse staging to achieve the 'skeletal' quality of the mythic story because, as Miller wrote, 'nothing existed but the purpose of the tale'. Even the character development was limited to advancing the tale, thus restricting the naturalistic acting style that still dominated the American stage.

When writing the two-act version, Miller enlarged the psychological motivations of the principal characters – Eddie, Beatrice and Catherine. He believed Eddie's action was made more understandable because he no longer concentrated only on the factual events of the tale. With the inclusion of additional dialogue to round out the characterisations of the three principal roles, the expanded version demanded two acts. Miller wrote in the Introduction to the two-act play that

> I felt it could now afford to include elements of simple human motivation – specifically the viewpoints of Eddie's wife, and *her* dilemma in relation to him. This in fact accounts for almost all the added material, which made it necessary to break the play in the middle for an intermission.

Miller decided to end Act One with the dramatic confrontation between Marco and Eddie when the once-compliant Marco shows his awareness of Eddie's threat to Rodolpho by holding the chair over Eddie's head. Act Two begins with the explosive scene when Eddie discovers Rodolpho and Catherine in the bedroom.

In revising the play, Miller also tried to show Eddie more closely in relation to the Sicilian-American society. He realised that 'The mind of Eddie Carbone is not comprehensible apart from its relation to his neighborhood, his fellow workers, his social situation. His self-esteem depends upon their estimate of him, and his value is created largely by his fidelity to the code of his culture.' In this production the set was more realistic. The pay-scale of the London theatre also allowed Miller to have several more actors playing Eddie's neighbours. Miller explained that in the New York production, there had only been four strategically placed actors to represent Eddie's community. In London, at least twenty men and women surrounded the main action. Miller ultimately judged that 'once Eddie had been placed squarely in his social context, among his people, the mythlike feeling of the story emerged of itself, and he could be made more human and less a figure, a force'. Moreover, 'the importance of his interior psychological dilemma was magnified to the size it would have in life. What had seemed like a mere aberration had now risen to a fatal violation of ancient law.' Twenty years later, in *Timebends*, Miller commented on how the revised staging also emphasised Eddie's universal destiny:

> The play began on a Red Hook street against the exterior brick wall of a tenement, which soon split open to show a basement apartment and above it a maze of fire escapes winding back and forth across the face of the building in the background. On those fire escapes the neighbors appeared at the end like a chorus, and Eddie could call up to them, to his society and his conscience for their support of his cause. Somehow, the splitting in half of the whole three-story tenement was awesome, and it opened the mind to the size of the mythic story. (431)

In the two-act version, Miller expanded the characterisation of Beatrice by focusing on her relationships with Eddie and Catherine. For example, there are substantial differences between the one-act and two-act versions of the play regarding the nature of Eddie and Beatrice's sexual relationship. The one-act version downplays Eddie's impotence, something that is central in the two-act version. The two-act version more vividly portrays Eddie and Beatrice's sex life when she asks him, 'When am I going to

be a wife again, Eddie?', which heightens the sexual
conflicts of the play. In Act Two, Miller also includes
dialogue in which Eddie speaks about his sex life: 'I want my
respect, Beatrice, and you know what I am talkin' about . . .
What I feel like doin' in the bed and what I don't feel like
doin' . . . I don't want no more conversations about that.'

Miller also added a scene in Act One which includes a
conversation between Beatrice and Catherine about her
relationship with Eddie. Miller portrays Beatrice as aware of
both Catherine's and Eddie's complex feelings. She realises
much more consciously than Catherine or Eddie does that
Catherine is a woman, and Beatrice tries to convey that to
her. Beatrice encourages Catherine to leave the house, to
marry Rodolpho and for them to find a place of their own.
She says, 'You're a woman, that's all, and you got a nice
boy, and now the time came when you said good-bye.'
When Catherine hesitates, Beatrice is firm: 'Honey . . . you
gotta.' Beatrice's action in this additional scene displays her
own complicated situation: torn between her devotion to
her husband, her own desires as a wife and the responsibility
for the girl she has raised as a daughter.

In *A View from the Bridge* Miller created the role of a
narrator, the lawyer Alfieri, who functions like a Greek
chorus: he is both a character and a commentator.
Although his original intention was to use Alfieri to convey
his own wonder when he first heard the tale of the
longshoreman, he clearly uses Alfieri's speeches to the
audience to connect Eddie to what Miller sees as the
mythic level of the play: Eddie's larger universal fate and
his destiny to enact the tragedy. Alfieri is also crucial in
showing the audience the significance of Eddie's actions to
himself, his family and his society. Miller's decision to use a
narrator in *A View from the Bridge* was perhaps influenced by
Thornton Wilder's use of the Stage Manager in *Our Town*
in 1938, and Tennessee Williams's successful use of Tom
Wingfield as the narrator in *The Glass Menagerie* in 1945.
Miller acknowledged the influence that both Wilder and
Williams had on the development of his stagecraft.

Themes

In *A View from the Bridge* sexuality, responsibility, betrayal and the law are intertwined with the psychological and social forces operating in the play.

Sexuality

The most provocative sexual issues *A View from the Bridge* raises are incest and homosexuality. Eddie's desire for his niece Catherine is at the centre of all the play's action. From the outset his attention to Catherine is depicted as more than fatherly affection. There are a number of intriguing twists to Eddie's desire for Catherine. Catherine is really Beatrice's niece whom Eddie has raised as his own daughter. And the fact that she is not his niece by blood further complicates Eddie's attraction to her. His need to protect her childhood innocence and virginity, first portrayed as fatherly affection, is put into a different light when he becomes enraged by her relationship with Rodolpho. His desire is evident when he reveals his disgust at Rodolpho putting his hands on her. Yet twice in the play Eddie is portrayed as unconscious of his desires. When he goes to see Alfieri for legal advice, the lawyer voices his concern for Eddie's inner turmoil. And at the end of the play Beatrice will similarly confront her husband by forcing him to face the reality he is unwilling or unable to acknowledge.

Catherine's interest in Rodolpho is obvious on the first night of their arrival. When Catherine and Rodolpho begin their relationship, Eddie's paternal concern turns into jealousy, which he uses to attack Rodolpho. Eddie is repulsed by what he perceives to be Rodolpho's effeminate nature, an unfamiliar form of masculinity. Eddie is especially alarmed that Catherine finds Rodolpho sexually attractive. Eddie tries to convince Catherine that Rodolpho is merely using her as a means to achieve American citizenship but his argument is actually a mask for Eddie's own desire for her.

Eddie's conflicted sexual impulses remain one of the most

intriguing aspects of the play. There are substantial differences between the original one-act version of the play and the revised two-act version regarding the nature of Eddie and Beatrice's physical relationship. Although he is unable to perform with Beatrice, he clearly desires Catherine, but at the same time he does not want her virginity violated. Furthermore, Eddie seems to be similarly attracted to Rodolpho, whose masculinity he assaults because he is both confused and repulsed by Rodolpho's behaviour. Nevertheless, Eddie perceives Rodolpho as a sexual threat. Eddie confuses sexual potency with a macho form of masculinity. He discovers that, in addition to singing and sewing, Rodolpho also cooks. Although he is told about the male chefs in European hotels, he does not appreciate a European view of what constitutes masculine behaviour. As a recently assimilated American, Eddie is uneasy about his own immigrant Italian culture. For him, masculinity is only physical strength and he challenges Rodolpho to a boxing match, knowing that he can overpower him.

Responsibility

Miller's plays concern themselves with the issue of characters accepting responsibility for their actions. Joe Keller in *All My Sons*, Willy Loman in *Death of a Salesman* and John Proctor in *The Crucible* struggle to accept and understand the consequences of their actions on themselves and others. At its core *A View from the Bridge* illustrates the complexity of accepting – or denying – full responsibility for one's actions and the effect this has on oneself, one's family and society. Eddie declares that Catherine 'is my niece and I'm responsible for her'. But Eddie perverts his responsibility to her and in the process violates the codes that bind him to his community. The consequences are tragic.

One of the most shocking aspects of Eddie's failure to fulfil his responsibility is that the play initially depicts him as fully aware of his role as surrogate father to Catherine, husband to Beatrice, willing host to Marco and Rodolpho, and member of his immigrant community. Although Miller was intrigued by the events of the story on which he based the play and wanted to illustrate the events as the work of fate, the playwright in Miller wanted to show that human beings are not merely victims of forces beyond their control. His characters determine their own destinies. Most of Eddie's actions are indeed purposeful – his attack on Rodolpho, the passionate kissing of Catherine, the demeaning kiss on Rodolpho's lips, the information he delivers to the Immigration Bureau. His failure is that he is never truly aware of the part he has played in the unfolding of these terrible events. Refusing to accept blame, he displays no guilt and accepts no responsibility, even when the catastrophe he has caused is pointed out to him. In contrast, Beatrice and Rodolpho clearly take full responsibility for the choices they have made.

Betrayal and Informing

From the perspective of Eddie's society, informing on Marco and Rodolpho to the immigration authorities is a heinous act. Although Eddie snitches for personal motives – to have Rodolpho deported and therefore eliminated from Catherine's life – he unwittingly commits an act of betrayal not only of his family but also of the larger circle of the immigrant society in which he lives. He makes his telephone call without knowing that Beatrice has arranged to move Marco and Rodolpho to an upstairs neighbour's apartment where other illegal immigrants are housed. His violation of what is in fact taboo becomes public when Marco accuses him before the gathered neighbours. As a result, Eddie becomes obsessed with his reputation. And it is his mania to maintain his dignity before his society that ultimately causes his death.

In *A View from the Bridge* Miller was also interested in exploring further the themes of betrayal and informing that he had previously illustrated in *The Crucible* in his response to McCarthyism and the naming of names before the House Committee on Un-American Activities. However, between writing the one-act version in 1955 and his revisions for the two-act version, Miller himself experienced the pressure to inform and betray when he, too, was called before HUAC in 1956 to 'name names'. Thus, his depiction of those who would 'call out' others in order to protect themselves is perhaps even more complicated than it is in *The Crucible*. Eddie Carbone is an amalgam of motives, emotions and unreconciled conflicts. Miller structures his play for us to witness and consider its multiple resonances. And as we do so, it is difficult to condemn Eddie without sympathy.

Law

A View from the Bridge represents a world in which legal, moral, ethical and social issues are in conflict with one another. Although Alfieri, as a lawyer, provides the interpretation of civil law, from his very first monologue he also shows that such law is not always a cultural precedent followed in the context of a Sicilian neighbourhood in Brooklyn. The law is not always clear nor does it satisfy basic instincts. Alfieri has witnessed men 'justly shot by unjust men'. The longshoremen of the play operate outside technical legality and sometimes consider illegal action 'just' in their code: harbouring illegal aliens is a sanctioned activity; the act of informing is abhorrent, a crime against the clan. Alfieri gives voice to these contradictions to both Eddie and Marco but he is powerless to prevent the law of the tribe from being enacted. As the play moves to its conclusion, we see how moral law is far more persuasive than civil law.

The scenes in Act One and Act Two when Eddie visits Alfieri's office forcefully present the contrast between the social, moral and legal codes that operate in the play. Eddie wants to prevent Catherine and Rodolpho's marriage because 'the guy ain't right'. But Alfieri tells him that 'morally and legally you have no rights'. Eddie fails to understand how Alfieri's explanation of civil law interprets natural law. As a lawyer, Alfieri functions under a code of modern American society which he describes in his very first commentary in the play as 'more civilized'. However, in

Alfieri's own words, Eddie is not connected to this civilised law; his nature harks back to his roots in the old world. Because Eddie has no legal recourse to stop Catherine and Rodolpho's relationship, he chooses to act according to his own code. Alfieri points out to him that he will drown if he violates the social and moral codes so powerful in his neighbourhood, especially the ethnic code he breaches by reporting Marco and Rodolpho. It is ironic that according to the code operating in Red Hook, Eddie is technically committing a crime by harbouring illegal aliens, but this action is permissible, even sanctioned in the community. Making the phone call to report illegal immigrants, according to civil law, is the proper action; however, the play illustrates that the moral law of the Italian society supersedes civil law – an action which makes Eddie an outcast.

The violation of this ethnic code is enforced in the scene between Alfieri and Marco after his arrest by immigration officials. Marco seeks revenge on Eddie because he has violated the Sicilian code based on loyalty to one's blood and family, and the violation exacts terrible consequences. As Marco says, 'In my country he would be dead now.' Alfieri is reluctant to bail out Marco unless he promises not to exact this revenge: 'To promise not to kill is not dishonourable.' Ironically, Marco has the same difficulty as Eddie in understanding how the civil law conflicts with his moral code:

Marco   Then what is to be done with such a man?
Alfieri   Nothing. If he obeys the law, he lives. That's all.
Marco (*rises, turns to* **Alfieri**)   The law? All the law is not in a book.
Alfieri   Yes. In a book. There is no other law.
Marco (*his anger rising*)   He degraded my brother – my blood. He robbed my children, he mocks my work. I work to come here, mister!
Alfieri   I know, Marco –
Marco   There is no law for that? Where is the law for that?

Alfieri   There is none.
Marco (*shaking his head, sitting*)   I don't understand this
country. (73)

Marco's frustration at the law not punishing Eddie shows
how the law is at odds with Marco's sense of justice. Here
'civilised' America undermines the ethnic code of Marco's
land, which abhors the violation of 'blood'. For Sicilians this
violation must be avenged, offering us another 'view' of how
justice has its say in different worlds.

Language

Miller wrote the one-act version in an intriguing mixture of
prose and verse; the expanded two-act version eliminated
the verse, but retained the characters speaking in a
colloquial idiom that actually disguises Miller's use of
metaphor.

Although Miller eliminated the verse lines in rewriting the
play, he retained a sophisticated use of poetic language.
Very little critical attention has been paid to the language of
Miller's dialogue. Throughout his career, Miller was subject
to reviews critical of the language of his plays. For example,
in a review in the *Nation* of the original production of *Death of
a Salesman*, Joseph Wood Krutch criticised the play for 'its
failure to go beyond literal meaning and its undistinguished
dialogue'. As a language stylist, Miller has been under-
appreciated, too often overshadowed by his contemporary,
Tennessee Williams, whose major strength as a dramatist
for many critics lies in the lyricism of his plays. Because
Miller was so often pigeonholed as a social dramatist, most
criticism focuses on the cultural relevance of his plays. Most
critics are content to regard his dialogue as 'colloquial',
judging that Miller used best what Leonard Moss described
as 'the common man's language' to reflect the social
concerns of his characters. The assumption is that most of
Miller's characters speak a realistic prose – a style that by
implication seems at first glance antithetical to poetic
language. However, Miller created a unique dramatic idiom

which undoubtedly marks him as a significant stylist nonetheless.

Although Miller works mostly in a form of colloquial prose, there are moments in his plays when the dialogue reaches for something more. He often takes the colloquialisms, clichés and idioms of everyday language and reveals the eloquence it can contain, especially in shifting words from their denotative to connotative meanings. Moreover, he employs the figurative devices of metaphor, symbol and imagery to give poetic significance to prose dialect. In many texts he embeds a series of metaphors – many are extended – which possess particular connotations in the societies in which individual plays are set. Most importantly, such figurative devices serve to support the tragic conflicts of the social themes that are the central focus of Miller's plays.

Indeed, poetic elements pervade the Miller canon. For example, in *All My Sons*, allusions, symbols and images place the themes of sacrifice and redemption in a religious context. In *Death of a Salesman* the extended metaphors of sports and business convey Willy Loman's struggle to achieve the American Dream in a capitalist economic system. In *The Crucible* poetic language illustrates the conflicts polarising the Salem community; images, symbols and metaphors, conceived in series of opposites, signify the Salemites' polarised view of a world of extremes. Heat and cold, white and black, light and dark, soft and hard connote the existence of the ultimate opposites: good and evil. In fact, Miller acknowledged that he was 'up to his neck' in writing many of his early full-length and radio plays in verse. When he graduated from the University of Michigan and started his work with the Federal Theatre Project in 1938, he wrote *The Golden Years*, a verse play about Montezuma. Later he explained that his first drafts for *Death of a Salesman* and all of *The Crucible* were written in verse. Miller regretted his failure to do this in *The American Clock*.

A View from the Bridge contains several poetic devices that heighten the conflicts and themes of the play. Consistent with Miller's use of language throughout his work, these poetic devices rely heavily on the tension between literal and figurative meanings, and they often include a high level of dramatic irony. Many of Alfieri's speeches to the audience at the beginning and end of scenes use figurative devices. In his opening monologue in Act One, he uses images of the sea and blood to connect the Brooklyn immigrant society to its roots in Sicily – especially Sicily of the past. He uses the sea of New York harbour to make this connection:

> But this is Red Hook, not Sicily. This is the slum that faces the bay on the seaward side of Brooklyn Bridge. This is the gullet of New York swallowing the tonnage of the world. And now we are quite civilized, quite American. (4)

Alfieri speaks of a case coming every few years that goes beyond the petty legal squabbles he usually arbitrates, and when he hears this kind of trouble

> The flat air in my office suddenly washes in with the green scent of the sea, the dust in this air is blown away and the thought comes that in some Caesar's year, in Calabria perhaps or on the cliff at Syracuse, another lawyer, quite differently dressed, heard the same complaint and sat there as powerless as I, and watched it run its bloody course. (4)

The images of sea and blood in this speech establish a number of parallels between the old and new worlds: the green scent of the sea in New York harbour echoes the Mediterranean sea surrounding Italy. And such images emblematise just how deeply rooted Eddie's fate is in a mythic past.

Alfieri's monologue ends with another sea image that reinforces Eddie's connection to an older world: 'This one's name was Eddie Carbone, a longshoreman working the docks from Brooklyn Bridge to the breakwater where the open sea begins.' Thus, the 'bridge' of the play's title gives us the 'view' for this story. From the Brooklyn Bridge one can see all the docks in Red Hook where Eddie works as a longshoreman. The metaphoric view, however, extends beyond the breakwater – because Eddie's destiny comes from Italy across the same luminous sea. The destiny of his ancestors spans a bridge between the old and new worlds. The span here further suggests the bridge of a ship, the lookout from which a ship is commanded as it sails between the two worlds.

Alfieri conveys that Eddie's case must run its 'bloody' course, an image that has a powerful literal and figurative meaning in the play. Miller emphasises this by repeating the narrator's statement a number of times, heightening the figurative use of language through the device of repetition. For Sicilians blood is the unifying factor in society, connecting the individual to his immediate family, as well as to his societal family. Eddie violates such blood relationships: he violates his paternal relation to Catherine; he violates his conjugal relationship with Beatrice; he violates Rodolpho's masculinity; and he fatally violates his immigrant society by informing on 'illegals' to the authorities. Both Marco and Eddie want to avenge their 'blood' and their vengeance operates literally and figuratively. As Marco says to Alfieri, 'He degraded my brother. My blood.'

At the play's climax, the image of blood is particularly effective. Rodolpho tries to make peace with Eddie before Marco comes for revenge, but Eddie refuses because he is furious at Marco for having sullied his name in front of the neighbourhood. When Eddie rebuffs Rodolpho, Beatrice says: 'Only blood is good? He kissed your hand!' Of course, Beatrice refers to the literal shedding of blood, the vendetta which may be avoided only by Eddie, Rodolpho and Marco's rapprochement. However, in the ensuing dialogue blood assumes an additional symbolic meaning:

Beatrice   You want somethin' else, Eddie, and you can never have her!
Catherine (*in horror*)   B!
Eddie (*shocked, horrified, his fists clenching*)   Beatrice!
Marco appears outside, walking toward the door from a distant point.

Beatrice (*crying out, weeping*)   The truth is not as bad as blood, Eddie! I'm tellin' you the truth – and tell her goodbye for ever!
Eddie (*crying out in agony*)   That's what you think of me – that I would have such thoughts? (77)

In this scene Beatrice refers to blood as 'bloodshed'. However, because she juxtaposes blood with the truth of Eddie's desire for Catherine, it assumes a figurative meaning as well. For Eddie's desire for Catherine is a violation of the blood that courses through his relationships with his family. His violation tragically severs the responsibility to his own blood.

The image of 'tunnels' is also significant, and Alfieri uses this more than once. In his commentary at the end of Act One, he describes Eddie's eyes 'like tunnels; my first thought was that he had committed a crime'. As Eddie moves towards his tragic fate, the light of his eyes indicates the tunnel in which he is trapped. Alfieri describes a passion which 'had moved into his body, like a stranger'. Of course, this passion has many meanings for Eddie: his desire for Catherine, his jealousy, his hatred – even attraction – for Rodolpho.

When Eddie returns to Alfieri's office in Act Two, the imagery of a tunnel stresses Eddie's march toward his fate. In his commentary Alfieri says: 'I will never forget how dark the room became when he looked at me; his eyes were like tunnels. I kept wanting to call the police, but nothing had happened.' This is a crucial scene because Alfieri's mention of a possible crime shows how the law works on several levels in the play: natural law, the Sicilian code and civil law. Eddie is about to snitch: the very act at the end of the dark tunnel when his tale has run its bloody course. Eddie's real tragedy is that he does not recognise the tunnel he is walking through.

In addition to the figurative language that Alfieri uses in his speeches, other images, symbols and metaphors are scattered throughout the play. These devices are rooted in the language of Sicilian-American society, a unique idiom expressing personal, familial, social, religious and cultural codes dictating an individual's behaviour and with which Eddie is in perilous conflict. Images, symbols and metaphors, among them the Madonna, angels and the innocence of a child appear throughout the play to indicate Eddie's struggle with these moral codes.

Eddie's awareness of Catherine's sexuality is often expressed by the iconic female image of the Madonna, the mother of Jesus. In Act One, Eddie first uses this religious allusion to convey his awe at Catherine's beauty:

> With your hair that way you look like a madonna, you know that? You're the madonna type. (*She doesn't look at him, but continues ladling out food onto the plates.*) You wanna go to work, heh, Madonna? (13)

The allusion works on many complicated levels in the text. The Madonna, as the mother of Jesus, possesses a purity, chastity and virginity that contrasts with the immoral sexual attractiveness which Eddie associates with high-heeled shoes and actresses. Eddie would like to preserve Catherine's chastity, which could be threatened by young men if she flaunts her physical beauty by wearing high heels and calling out of windows. In Act One, Eddie repeats his concern for Catherine's chastity when he warns Rodolpho that he does not want her to go to Times Square because 'it's full of tramps over there'. Yet Eddie's wish to keep Catherine's virginity intact is juxtaposed by his physical desire for her, which ironically would destroy her purity. His physical urge is clearly indicated later in the play when he kisses her passionately in Act Two. The Madonna image has powerful religious connections for Italians, which expands Eddie's violation of his cultural codes still further. For not only does Eddie's violation of Catherine, as her surrogate father, border on incest, his violation of her as a Madonna figure is also a grievous sin.

The Madonna image also has powerful psychological connotations in the play. Normally applied to a husband's feelings for his wife, the so-called 'Madonna Complex' operates in an intriguing manner in *A View from the Bridge*.

Eddie obviously possesses potent feelings for Catherine that
resemble the Madonna complex; however, Eddie and
Beatrice's marriage bears scrutiny in this vein. Eddie's
inability to sleep with Beatrice may be explained easily by
the Madonna complex, but his sexual feelings are
complicated. Moreover, the Madonna complex maintains
that a husband's sexual inadequacy with his wife occurs as a
result of her becoming a mother. The one-act and two-act
plays offer different versions of this. In the one-act play,
Eddie and Beatrice have two children; in the two-act play,
references to the children have been cut. This editing has a
powerful effect on how we read the images. Because
Beatrice and Eddie are childless in the two-act version, they
have put all their parental feelings into Catherine. In a
sense, this magnifies Eddie's incestuous attraction. And
because Eddie is so consumed with Rodolpho's masculinity,
his own infertility somehow magnifies his inadequacy,
especially for a man from a macho Italian culture.

Another image, used both literally and figuratively, is that
of riding. In Act One, Rodolpho romantically and
humorously describes how he pushes taxis and horse
carriages up the hill in his Italian home town, and how he
desires to own a motorcycle so he can become a messenger.
Such modes of transport become figurative in the next scene
when Eddie and Beatrice await Rodolpho and Catherine's
return from a date. Eddie is worried that 'he's takin' her for
a ride', a slang term for taking advantage of her that
includes significant sexual connotations. Moreover,
Beatrice's response, 'All right, that's her ride', is ironic since
she senses Eddie's desire for her niece. Eddie's sexual
feelings for Catherine are challenged by Rodolpho, and for
Catherine to become Rodolpho's, he must take her for the
metaphorical ride, not Eddie.

The image of riding continues in the same context later in
the play when Eddie tells Catherine his suspicion that
Rodolpho is only 'bowin' to his passport'. Eddie describes
him as 'a hit-and-run guy, baby; he's got bright lights in his
head, Broadway'. With the 'hit-and-run guy' image, Eddie
vividly depicts Rodolpho as a driver intent on running down

Catherine's chastity, then leaving the scene. However, when Catherine denies this, Eddie says, 'He could be picked up any day here and he's back pushin' taxis up the hill.' Ironically Eddie applies the literal meaning to the image, exhibiting how Miller can create significant tension between the denotative and connotative meaning of his words.

Eddie's conversation with Alfieri in his law office in Act One contains many images with various negative and positive connotations about women, all of which connect to indicate Eddie's growing crisis and conflicted feelings towards Catherine and Rodolpho. Early in the play Eddie has made references to actresses, chorus girls, high-heeled shoes, stereotypical blondes and the film star Greta Garbo to describe the types of women he does not want Catherine to emulate because of the way they flaunt their sexuality. His desire to preserve Catherine's chastity is clear from the outset of the play. He does not like Catherine to wear high-heeled shoes because he associates high-heeled shoes with the kind of shoes worn by actresses in the movies and, perhaps, with whores in Sicily. Eddie obviously associates movie actresses with female immorality. The image of shoes reveals his actual concern with the sexual allure they give, and Eddie's desire for Catherine is at the core of this allure. Eddie does not want Catherine desired by other men like some Garbo-esque, screen-star icon. He does not want her to attract sexual attention, as he says, 'You're walkin' wavy.' Eddie attempts to suppress Catherine's budding sexuality; ironically, he not only notices it, but is enticed by it. Yet his physical attraction to her is a violation of one of the supreme moral codes at the centre of this play.

In his attempt to feminise Rodolpho, Eddie describes Rodolpho's blond hair as 'platinum', which echoes his previous descriptions of women. Eddie also says about Rodolpho: 'I mean if you close the paper fast – you could blow him over.' This recalls Rodolpho's rendition of 'Paper Doll' and his previous complaint to Beatrice about the dockworkers' nickname. In emasculating Rodolpho, Eddie figuratively attempts to make him into a paper doll.

Eddie uses a particularly revealing image when he describes Rodolpho sewing a dress for Catherine: 'I mean he looked so sweet there, like an angel – you could kiss him he was so sweet.' The angel comparison echoes many of the previous images and allusions. Certainly an angel recalls the Madonna image, for an angel typically possesses the same whiteness and purity. Moreover, traditionally angels are often depicted as blonde and sexless. Yet the angel imagery also shows the complicated nature of Eddie's feelings for Rodolpho. Eddie ironically reveals the same attraction to Rodolpho as he does towards Catherine. The angel image connotes the same sanctity as the Madonna image, both of which are juxtaposed with the physical desire, culminating in a kiss. Although he attempts to emasculate Rodolpho, Eddie paradoxically perceives him as a sexual threat, as when he says, 'When I think of that guy layin' his hands on her I could –.' However, Eddie has confused sexuality and masculinity. Blind to his own desires, he merely sees Rodolpho as a criminal: 'He takes and puts his dirty filthy hands on her like a goddam thief.' Eddie's blindness is indicated when Alfieri says, 'She can't marry you, can she?' and he furiously replies, 'What are you talkin' about, marry me! I don't know what the hell you're talkin' about!' Ironically, the initial use of 'angel' in the play is when Beatrice describes Eddie in the very first scene as an 'angel' for agreeing to take her cousins in as illegal boarders.

Finally, the play consistently uses terms like 'baby', 'little girl' and 'big girl' to describe Catherine. In the first scene of the play, Eddie tells Catherine, 'You're a baby, you don't understand these things.' He then says, 'You're gettin' to be a big girl now.' Beatrice repeatedly addresses her niece as 'baby', but argues with Eddie when he is reluctant to allow her to take the secretarial job, saying 'She's no baby no more' – indicating the essence of the conflict. Eddie, almost in tears after giving her permission to work, laments, 'I guess I just never figured on one thing . . . That you would ever grow up.'

Characters

Eddie

Eddie Carbone is one of Arthur Miller's more complicated and puzzling protagonists. After writing the one-act version of the play Miller said that the meaning of Eddie's fate still remained a mystery to him. Concerned about telling the 'myth-like march of the tale' without embellishment, Miller remained unsettled by Eddie's tragedy. In revising the play for its two-act version, Miller thought that the addition of significant psychological and behavioural details, including Beatrice's and Catherine's viewpoints, would render the play not only more human, warmer and less remote, but also provide a 'clearer statement'. Miller noted that the two-act play made it 'more possible now to relate [Eddie's] actions to our own and thus to understand ourselves a little better not only as psychological entities, but as we connect to our fellows and our long past together.'

Eddie's complex personality manifests itself in a series of contradictory actions that violate the codes by which he lives. We are shocked and appalled by much of what he does: his feelings for Catherine are nothing if not incestuous, and his disregard for Beatrice violates their marriage vows. His attack on Rodolpho involves several motives, and his betrayal of the cousins to the immigration authorities is inexcusable.

Yet Alfieri clearly judges that 'he was a good a man as he had to be in a life that was hard and even'. This goodness must be considered in any evaluation of his character. He has raised Catherine, he agrees to put up the 'submarines' who are, after all, Beatrice's cousins not his, just as Catherine is Beatrice's biological niece. He is a decent provider and a hard worker. There is even a reference to Beatrice having taken in relatives after her father's house burned down, causing Eddie to sleep on the floor. He is genuinely moved by the prospect of taking in the 'submarines', even while acknowledging the substantial legal risks this involves.

All of his actions in the play are motivated by what he believes are the best interests of Catherine. His concern about her safety in a new job and her attractiveness to young men seems initially appropriate and paternal. Nor is he portrayed as intractable: he gives in to Beatrice's and Catherine's pleas and allows her to take the job she is offered. His sense of duty is laudable: he promised Catherine's mother on her deathbed to raise her and he has. All of this kindness is compromised when he is unwilling, indeed unable, to see any other point of view once he sets himself the task of protecting Catherine.

Alfieri describes a passion that 'had moved into his body, like a stranger'. Eddie Carbone is a man in whom passion outweighs reason. He does not understand his desire, even when it is pointed out to him. When Alfieri suspects that Eddie is on the verge of an act of betrayal, he warns him of the consequences: 'You won't have a friend in the world, Eddie! Even those who understand will turn against you . . . Put it out of your mind!' Despite the warning, Eddie makes his fateful telephone call. He doesn't even seem to recognise the impulse that leads to his kissing Rodolpho.

One way to understand Eddie is to see him in the context of his culture. Revising the play for the London version, Miller sought to place Eddie squarely in relation to the cultural codes of his Sicilian-American environment of Red Hook in the mid-1950s. Eddie's world is insular, personal, familial, social and religious. For the transplanted Sicilians, these are the unifying factors that determine their relationship to the docks and the streets of their neighbourhood, even to their own homes. When Eddie crosses these boundaries he is doomed.

Eddie belongs to a long line of Miller characters who want to protect the dignity of their names. In Miller's first Broadway hit *All My Sons* (1947), Joe Keller's pride as a self-made businessman is proclaimed in the sign over his warehouse. In *Death of a Salesman*, Willy Loman's search for dignity is part of the play's climax: 'I am Willy Loman and you are Biff Loman.' In *The Crucible*, John Proctor refuses to let his signed confession be posted on the Salem church door: 'Because it is my name.' In *A View from the Bridge*, Eddie Carbone similarly wants his good name back. Although Alfieri's final monologue mourns him, 'I admit it – with a certain . . . alarm', Miller said that 'Eddie is still not a man to weep over'.

Eddie's situation in the play can be tied to Miller's original intention of telling the tale as a Greek myth, linking the protagonist's story to ancient, even savage, roots. Are not myth and legend our struggle to explain inexplicable dark human desires and instincts? Aristotle tells us to pity and fear, pity out of human compassion and fear because the same fate can happen to all of us. Miller believed that the two-act play made it 'more possible now to relate [Eddie's] actions to our own and thus to understand ourselves a little better not only as psychological entities, but as we connect to our fellows and our long past together'. As a tragic figure Eddie cries out for personal dignity, even though he is in wrongful pursuit of a dignity he has himself never really understood.

Beatrice

Beatrice is depicted as the devoted wife of Eddie and mother figure to Catherine. Her genuine goodness and generosity is shown by how she has raised Catherine, her sister's child. Initially in the play, Beatrice's character seems stereotypical: she is concerned about the cooking and the cleanliness of the apartment. She exhibits the appropriate deference to Eddie as husband and man of the house, seeking his permission and approval for Catherine's job and her cousins' stay in the apartment. She genuinely means it when she calls him an angel and proclaims that he will be blessed for his good deeds.

However, this is not to suggest that Beatrice is a flat, one-dimensional character. She has considerable depth and complexity and the ability to respond sensibly to the conflicts that erupt when her cousins arrive. Beatrice is often a mediator. At the beginning of the play she successfully convinces Eddie that Catherine, now seventeen, is no longer

a child and that he must let her grow up. When Eddie
objects to Catherine and Rodolpho's growing relationship,
Beatrice tries to persuade him that it is time he let her go. In
the final scene of Act One, she is particularly adept at
reading the tension between Eddie, Rodolpho and
Catherine; she encourages Rodolpho and Catherine to
dance, gently probes Marco about his wife, moderates
Eddie's scoffing at Rodolpho and questions why Eddie
needs to teach Rodolpho to box. In Act Two she makes the
arrangements to move Rodolpho and Marco to another
apartment.

Beatrice is perceptive about the complexity of Eddie and
Catherine's relationship. She is aware of both Catherine's
and Eddie's complex feelings for one another. Her
dimension as a character is also evident in the way Miller
depicts Beatrice and Eddie's sexual relationship in the two-
act play. Beatrice has needs and desires of her own. She
needs Catherine out of the household in order to preserve
her own marriage. Catherine's sexual maturity coincides
with Eddie's apparent impotence. Beatrice wants her
husband back as a lover but Eddie's physical attraction to
Catherine interferes with Beatrice's sex life.

Ultimately Beatrice chooses to side with her husband
when Eddie won't allow her to attend Catherine's wedding.
However, in the climactic scene when Catherine tells Eddie
that he belongs in the garbage, Beatrice shows enormous
awareness of the role they all share in the tragedy, declaring:
'Then we all belong in the garbage. You and me, too. Don't
say that. Whatever happened we all done it, and don't you
ever forget it, Catherine.' She is the only one who
understands the responsibility they all share in the events
that unfold.

Catherine

Catherine is a character who develops her own strength
during the course of the play. In the first scenes, she conveys
an innocence that belies her seventeen years. She is
compliant and deferential, particularly to Eddie. Yet the

play begins exactly at the moment when Catherine is coming of age, and she is aware of her budding femininity and womanhood. Her desire to take a secretarial job indicates her search for the independence of adulthood. She is clearly devoted to Eddie, her surrogate father, and still seeks his permission, approval and affirmation in most aspects of her life.

Her change from child to adult is swift. Initially her innocence is evident in her awe at Rodolpho's blond hair and her naïve questions about life in Italy. She is immediately attracted to him but once they establish a serious relationship, she begins her separation from Eddie, the centre of the play's conflict. In the scene when Eddie suggests that Rodolpho is only using her to obtain a passport, she rejects his suggestion: 'I don't believe it and I wish to hell you'd stop it.' The final scene of Act One, when Catherine purposefully and provocatively dances with Rodolpho, is the final physical manifestation of her selfhood as a woman.

The first scene of Act Two is crucial. In Catherine's conversation with Rodolpho she shows a sensitivity to Eddie's needs as a man, and a remarkable perception that Beatrice does not provide for them. Underlying Catherine's speech is the suggestion of sexual awareness. Her own sexual needs will be fulfilled by Rodolpho. Catherine is even complicit in the loss of her virginity; she initiates their lovemaking when she says to Rodolpho 'teach me . . . I don't know anything', underlining also her inexperience. Catherine and Rodolpho's awareness of their own sexuality magnifies even further the shock of Eddie's kiss, which occurs moments later. Just before this occurs, Catherine expresses an awareness of her newly found maturity when she says, 'Eddie, I'm not gonna be a baby any more.' The image of her as a baby contrasts sharply with her physical experience as a woman. Eddie's kiss is therefore dramatic – the physical sign of his struggle to love her as a child/baby and desire her as a woman.

Rodolpho

Rodolpho is the younger of the two 'submarines' and his role in the play is in contrast to that of his brother Marco in many ways. With no family in Italy to support, he has no responsibilities and has come to indulge himself in the American dream of opportunity. He has the idealism and spirit of youth and sees possibilities in all things. He enjoys life and loves to share his joy with others. The playwright details the generous spirit of this blond Italian: his singing in the hotel in Italy, cooking for the men at sea, singing on the Red Hook docks – all of which Eddie neither appreciates nor understands. Rodolpho proclaims his intention to become an American citizen and return to Italy a rich man. Catherine is immediately attracted to Rodolpho's *joie de vivre* and he is equally attracted to her. Their young love is genuine – a result of his awe at this new world of New York with its movies, theatres and night life, and her wonder at the cultural difference of Rodolpho's life in Italy, with its lemons, fountains and old-world charm.

Like Catherine, Rodolpho is subject to change. He possesses a seriousness which tempers his natural inclination to be fun-loving, and he exhibits appropriate deference to and respect for Eddie, who has taken him in. The turning point in Rodolpho's development comes in the final scene of Act One which occurs late one evening after dinner. Eddie questions Marco about the sexual fidelity of wives back in Italy; he does this to emphasise to both Marco and Rodolpho that American girls like Catherine are not sexually 'easy'. He again complains about Rodolpho's lack of respect in keeping Catherine out late. Marco initially reinforces Eddie's position by telling Rodolpho that he must obey his host. When Catherine asks Rodolpho to dance, he agrees to do so only reluctantly, for he fears Eddie's reaction. Eddie seethes as he watches the couple engage in this most basic of mating rituals. Eddie reacts by coaxing Rodolpho into a boxing match, intended as an aggressive display of his superior physical strength in his own territory. Eddie strikes a staggering blow. The fight ends and Eddie seems satisfied – for the moment. But then a defiant

Rodolpho immediately turns to Catherine and asks her to dance, a direct challenge to Eddie's authority as well as his perceived physical strength.

Rodolpho's true character emerges in the final scene of the play. Despite the way Eddie has treated him, he warns him that Marco is coming to wreak vengeance. Rodolpho takes responsibility for his wrongdoing, wishes to apologise and even goes so far as to kiss Eddie's hand in deference, proclaiming, 'I have made all our troubles.' Clearly, Rodolpho, steeped in the Italian mores more than Eddie, understands the coming confrontation with Marco can only result in bloodshed.

Marco

As opposed to the younger Rodolpho, Marco is the serious, dark and brooding brother. He has come to America because the poor economic conditions of post-war Italy have made it difficult for him to support his wife and three children, one of whom is seriously ill. Marco is grateful and appropriately deferential to Eddie, and he often reminds Rodolpho to display the same respect. Marco's situation is made clear on the first night he arrives. He is moved to tears when he realises that he will immediately find work on the docks and can begin to send money back to his wife right away. He offers his hand in thanks to Eddie. In contrast to the entertainment Rodolpho provides on the piers (according to his fellow longshoremen), Marco works like a bull unloading cargo ships.

Marco is nonetheless a force to be reckoned with, especially when crossed. This is exhibited at the conclusion of Act One when Eddie defeats Rodolpho in the boxing match. Eddie has his own tactic turned on him when Marco challenges him to life one leg of a chair with a single hand and Eddie is unable to do so. By raising the chair over Eddie's head, Marco conveys a threat to Eddie: that he will protect his brother, his blood, should Eddie overstep the line again. His action foreshadows his challenge to Eddie at the end of the play.

Alfieri

Miller's plays are full of references to jail, crime and the law. Several of his plays contain lawyers either as major or minor characters. The most notable examples are George Deever in *All My Sons*, Bernard in *Death of a Salesman*, Danforth in *The Crucible*, Quentin in *After the Fall* and Tom Wilson in *The Ride Down Mount Morgan*. In Miller such figures often serve to elevate the moral crisis at the heart of a particular play.

Alfieri in *A View from the Bridge* is the moral arbiter of the law. He plays a dual role, functioning as both narrator and participant in the action. As the narrator of the play, he comments on the action and the audience is meant to view the events through Alfieri's eyes. Alfieri could be said to establish the 'view' to which the play's title refers. His opening monologue indicates that he acts in many ways as a 'bridge': he is a bridge between the old and new worlds, a bridge between the audience and the action, and a bridge between the various characters.

However, this is not meant to suggest that we should make the same judgments as Alfieri does. For he, too, clearly must be seen as a member of the Sicilian-American culture in which he lives. He readily acknowledges the status that his legal profession gives him in the Brooklyn neighbourhood. Unlike Eddie, Beatrice and Catherine, he was born in Italy: he is a genuine immigrant who truly understands the connections between the old and new world. As narrator he signals the importance and dimension of Eddie Carbone's story and he struggles hard to understand Eddie's actions and fate. Eddie is more than a client – for Alfieri he represents something almost larger than life itself.

As a participant in the action of the play, Alfieri is both father-confessor and arbiter of the law. Miller gives him three important scenes: with Eddie in his office in Act One, again with Eddie in his office in Act Two and in the detention centre offering advice to Marco. In his role as a lawyer, Alfieri represents American civil law, but he is also crucial in showing how civil law and its justice conflict with the morals operating in the Sicilian-American society.

Productions

American and English stage productions
The one-act version of *A View from the Bridge* opened on
Broadway on 29 September 1955 at the Coronet Theatre
(now the Eugene O'Neill Theatre) in a double-bill with *A
Memory of Two Mondays*. Directed by Martin Ritt, the cast
included Van Heflin as Eddie, Eileen Heckart as Beatrice,
Gloria Marlowe as Catherine, Jack Warden as Marco and
Richard Davalos as Rodolpho. The set was designed by
Boris Aronson and the production ran for 149
performances.

The relatively short run for *A View from the Bridge* was
disappointment for Miller, following the equally short run of
The Crucible in 1953. The reviews were mixed. Brooks
Atkinson recognised that the play had enough powerful
material for a 'forceful drama', but concluded that it did not
quite measure up to the level of tragedy. Despite such
reviews, Miller won his third Drama Desk Award.

Miller recognised that he was not fully focused on the
production. Distracted by his relationship with Marilyn
Monroe and his impending divorce, he remembered that he
could not concentrate during the casting calls. He assumed
that good actors could play most of the roles; he realised
later that some of the actors were miscast. Van Hefin's
preoccupation with conveying the mannerisms and speaking
in accents of an Italian longshoreman kept him from
'feeling' his part as Eddie. J. Carrol Nash was equally
troubled with portraying Alfieri. Miller also recognised that
he had not fully explored the roles Eddie, Catherine and
Beatrice play and, their parts underwritten, they seemed to
appear in an 'academic and irrelevant story of revenge'
(*Timebends*, 354).

Miller revised the play into its two-act for the London
production where it was first performed at the New
Watergate Club at the Comedy Theatre on 11 October
1956. The cast featured Anthony Quayle as Eddie, Mary
Ure as Catherine, Megs Jenkins as Beatrice, Brian Bedford
as Rodolpho, Ian Bannen as Marco, Richard Harris as

Louis and Michael Gwynn as Alfieri. The play opened only after some considerable controversy. The Lord Chamberlain refused to grant permission for *A View from the Bridge* to be performed because he considered a homosexual theme was inappropriate for the public good. The producers came up with the solution of making the audience members of the Comedy Theatre's New Watergate Club as part of their ticket price. The production was therefore considered private and could be performed without any restrictions.

The reviews of the London production were enthusiastic. The *Guardian*'s Philip Hope-Wallace called it 'deathly earnest'. Kenneth Tynan declared the play 'just short of being a masterpiece', and he found Peter Brook's production 'uncannily good'. The *Daily Mail*'s Cecil Wilson said that the play was 'savage, searing and spellbinding', Quayle giving 'the performance of his life'.

In casting for the London production, Miller was concerned, as he was in New York, with the ability of the actors, this time British, to speak with the deep Sicilian-American accents required for realistic characterisation. Quayle and Ure worked out an accent which Miller described as 'never heard on earth before', but they did convince London audiences that they were speaking Brooklynese. Under Peter Brooks's direction, *A View from Bridge* became in Miller's words, 'a heroic play of great emotional force, the working-class characters larger than life, grand and rather strange' (*Timebends*, 431).

The American premiere of the two-act version took place in 1965 in a successful off-Broadway production at the Sheridan Square Playhouse in New York. The play opened on 28 January and ran for 780 performances. Robert Duval starred as Eddie Carbone and Jon Voight played Rodolpho. The show was produced and directed by Ulu Grosbard, and Dustin Hoffman, who played Willy Loman in the 1984 Broadway revival of *Death of a Salesman*, was the assistant director. The play won two Obie Awards, for Distinguished Performance by Duval and Best Direction by Grosbard.

Miller felt that this production 'magically' caught the play's 'spirit'. Duvall said that Eddie Carbone was his

favourite role and *A View from the Bridge* the 'greatest play':
'People tend to overlook it. It's my Othello – as great a part,
to me, as Othello.' The reviews were enthusiastic: 'Robert
Duvall realizes the role of Eddie, the longshoreman whose
protective love of his niece turns incestuous, more
completely, I think, than any actor who's ever played it,'
wrote Norman Nadel in the *New York World-Telegram and Sun*
(29 January 1965). In the *New York Post* of the same date
Richard Watts wrote, 'In the crucial role of the embittered
Eddie, Robert Duvall is especially fine in suggesting the
attempted sense of fun in a man totally without it.'

The two-act version of *A View from the Bridge* did not have
its Broadway premiere until 1983. Directed by Arvin Brown
and starring Tony LoBianco as Eddie, the play opened on 3
February 1983 at the Ambassador Theater, where it
repeated the 1955 run of the one-act version of 149
performances before closing on 12 June. The reviews were
glowing. Frank Rich in the *New York Times* described it as a
'stunning revival . . . a much-needed evening of electric
American drama'. He praised 'the shrewd and forceful
direction of Arvin Brown and the tumultuous star
performance of Tony LoBianco'. The production won the
1983 Tony Award for Best Revival of a Play.

In 1987 Alan Ayckbourn directed a major London revival
at the National Theatre. The play opened on 12 February
1987 at the Cottesloe, and transferred to the Aldwych
Theatre in London's West End on 3 November 1987,
closing its year-long run on 20 February 1988.

Michael Gambon's portrayal of Eddie Carbone and
Ayckbourn's direction received universal praise among the
London critics. 'In any critic's life there are certain red-
letter nights. The new production of *A View from the Bridge* at
the Cottesloe is empathetically one of them. In the first
place it shows Michael Gambon shaking hands with
greatness. But Alan Ayckbourn's immaculately detailed
production also banishes any doubts about Arthur Miller's
play and vindicates its claim to be a modern tragedy'
(*Guardian*, 14 February 1987). 'It remains one of the great
productions of our time not only because of Michael

Gambon's towering central performance but because
Ayckbourn establishes the vital Miller connection between
the tragic hero and the moral laws of the tribal community'
(*Guardian*, 5 November 1987). 'It is hard to believe that there
ever has been, or perhaps ever will be, a better production
of Arthur Miller's *A View from the Bridge*' (*Punch*, 18
November 1987). Gambon won the 1983 Olivier Award for
Best Actor.

Another major Broadway revival opened on 14
December 1997 at the Criterion Center Stage Right in a
Roundabout Theatre Company production that later
transferred to the Neil Simon Theatre. Directed by Michael
Mayer, the cast included Anthony LaPaglia as Eddie,
Allison Janney as Beatrice, Brittany Murphy as Catherine
and Stephen Spinella as Alfieri. The production ran for 239
performances and won the Tony Award for Best Revival of
a Play; LaPaglia won the Tony Award for Best Actor in a
Play. The production also received the Drama Desk Award
for Outstanding Revival of a Play, Outstanding Featured
Actress in a Play for Janney, and Outstanding Direction of a
Play for Mayer. The reviews were enthusiastic. Ben Brantley
in the *New York Times* described the production as a 'first-
rate new revival . . . with a cast that approaches perfection
. . . Under Mr Mayer's finely calibrated direction, this
production seems to meet every requisite Mr Miller might
desire. The correlation with classical tragedy is directly
evoked by David Gallo's amphitheatre-inspired set, with
curved tiers of steps overlooking the circle where the
principal action takes place. The sense of a judgmental
community, which Mr Miller insists is central to the play, is
vividly embodied by the large ensemble of extras who fill the
stage between scenes. And Kenneth Posner's shadowy
lighting seems to locate the emotions the characters often
don't dare express.'

Another major London revival opened on 5 February
2009 at the Duke of York's Theatre, directed by Lindsay
Posner. The production featured Ken Stott as Eddie, Mary
Elizabeth Mastrantonio as Beatrice, Hayley Atwell as
Catherine and Harry Lloyd as Rodolpho. It closed on

16 May 2009. Michael Billington in the *Guardian* described
it as a 'perfectly decent production' but noted that Posner
'treats the play as the tragedy of a doomed individual',
rather than 'a portrait of a community'. He took issue with
Christopher Oram's design, 'dominated by a massive
tenement providing little space for the teeming street life of
Red Hook'. Lizzie Loveridge (*Curtain Up*) was, however,
more favourably impressed: 'With the experience of
Lindsay Posner and talented actors Ken Stott and Mary
Elizabeth Mastrantonio in the lead roles, there is very little
that can go wrong.' She, too, saw this production as
focusing on the tragedy of an individual: 'Here Eddie
Carbone is an isolated figure, head of his own family rather
than a member of the wider Italian American community.'
Benedict Nightingale of *The Times* wrote that, 'Lindsay
Posner's fine revival goes far towards convincing me that
Miller was right to believe he'd written a tragedy, complete
with a flawed protagonist.'

A much anticipated Broadway revival of *A View from the
Bridge* opened on 24 January 2010 at New York's Cort
Theatre, directed by the veteran Gregory Mosher. Tony
Award-winner and film star Liev Schreiber returned to the
Broadway stage as Eddie, the accomplished Jessica Hecht
was cast as Beatrice, and movie star Scarlett Johansson
made her Broadway debut as Catherine. The production
received universal rave reviews. John Lahr of *The New Yorker*
described the production as 'a singular astonishment: a kind
of theatrical lightning bolt that sizzles and startles . . . one of
the best productions of [Miller's] work that I've ever seen.'
Ben Brantley of the *New York Times* judged that Schreiber's
conception of Eddie 'registers changes in emotional
temperature with organic physical precision.' He also noted
that Johansson 'melts into her character so thoroughly that
her nimbus of celebrity disappears.' Joe Dziemianowicz of
the *New York Daily News* singled out Hecht as giving a
'performance of quiet anguish that ultimately erupts into
something shattering.'

Film adaptations

Luchino Visconti directed a stage version of *A View from the Bridge* in Italy in 1958. At the same time, he was working on his film *Rocco and his Brothers*, shot in 1960 and released the next year. The film is about an impoverished widow and her five sons, who migrate from a small southern Italian village in search of a better life in Milan. Critics at once recognised the strong influence of *A View from the Bridge* on Visconti's film.

A film directly based on *A View from the Bridge*, titled *Vu du pont*, was released in February 1961. The two-year run of the French stage production convinced the producer Paul Graetz that a movie version would be successful in the so-called 'art-house circuit' popular in the United States and Western Europe. Graetz shot the film simultaneously in English and French. He chose an American, Sidney Lumet, to direct. Exterior scenes were filmed on the streets of New York, and interior scenes in a Paris studio. The film featured a notable cast: Raf Vallone, who starred in the Paris stage production, reprised his role as Eddie. Maureen Stapleton, the renowned stage and screen actress, played Beatrice; Carol Lawrence, widely known for her role as Maria in the original Broadway production of *West Side Story*, was Catherine. Miller's friend, Michigan classmate and fellow playwright Norman Rosten wrote the screenplay. The film, however, opened to mixed reviews, some praising Lumet's superb direction and others describing it as bankrupt of vision. Some felt that the film was unclear on whether the events were naturalistic or tragic.

Opera

In 1999 an opera of *A View from the Bridge* with music by William Bolcom and libretto by Arnold Weinstein and Arthur Miller premiered at the Lyric Opera of Chicago.

The gestation for the opera version of *A View from the Bridge* began with Weinstein, who had taught the play in his classes at Columbia University. After Bolcom wrote the music for Miller's play *Broken Glass* in 1994, Weinstein, with

Miller's approval, encouraged him to make *A View from the Bridge* his next operatic project.

The work was performed in New York at the Metropolitan Opera in 2002. Bolcom made changes for the New York version, most notably adding two new arias, one each for the characters of Eddie and Beatrice. The New York production premiered on 5 December and received strong reviews. Howard Kissel of the *New York Daily News* judged it as 'one of those rare times when opera is great theater'. Anthony Tommasini of the *New York Times* called it an 'involving and significant work'. The New York production was given a total of eight performances and the final performance on 28 December 2002 was broadcast live over the Chevron Texaco Metropolitan Opera International Radio Network to more than 360 stations in the United States and forty countries around the world.

The production was widely praised for its strong performances: Kim Josephson's robust portrayal of Eddie strongly conveyed his tragic downfall; Catherine Malfitano's vocal range was particularly effective in capturing Beatrice's conflict between her niece and her husband; Isabel Bayrakdarian, in her Met debut, convincingly expressed Catherine's growth from girl to woman. Gregory Turay was outstanding as Rodolpho; his tenor voice frequently moved the audience to applause. His performance of 'New York Lights', when Rodolpho sings a paean about his love for New York City in the first act, is one of the more dramatic moments in the opera. The song received particular notice from music critics as a melody that could be attractive to popular music listeners. Bolcom explained that he conceived the piece as a fusion of Broadway melody and early-twentieth-century Neapolitan songs and the lyrics also mix images from Sicily and New York.

The massive set, designed by Santo Loquasto, who had previously designed the sets and costumes for Miller's 1994 play *Broken Glass*, merged the interior and exterior settings without clear delineation. Steel girders and platforms evoked both the docks where Eddie plied his trade as a longshoreman and the Brooklyn Bridge, with its literal and

figurative importance in the work. Brick and wood
suggested the tenement buildings of the Red Hook
neighbourhood. Scrims and projection screens on the back
walls of the stage showed images of Sicily, Brooklyn,
Manhattan and the Red Hook docks. The set provided the
necessary space for the production's large chorus. The
chorus, of course, fits Miller's grand scheme to place Eddie
among his neighbours in the large Sicilian-American
community.

In writing the libretto, Miller incorporated a significant
amount of the prose poetry belonging to the original one-act
version of *View*, adapting lyrical dialogue to the conventions
of operatic music. Since its premiere *A View from the Bridge* has
become a regular part of the American operatic repertoire,
playing at the Washington National Opera in 2007.

Further Reading

Works by Miller

Arthur Miller: Plays, 6 vols, with introductions by Arthur
  Miller (vol. 1: *All My Sons, Death of a Salesman, The Crucible,
  A Memory of Two Mondays, A View from the Bridge*; vol. 2: *The
  Misfits, After the Fall, Incident at Vichy, The Price, Creation of the
  World, Playing for Time*; vol. 3: *The American Clock, The
  Archbishop's Ceiling, Two-Way Mirror*; vol. 4: *The Golden
  Years, The Man Who Had All the Luck, I Can't Remember
  Anything, Clara*; vol. 5: *The Last Yankee, The Ride Down Mount
  Morgan, Almost Everybody Wins*; vol. 6: *Broken Glass, Mr
  Peters' Connections, Resurrection Blues, Finishing the Picture*).
  London: Methuen, 1988–2009
Collected Plays 1944–1961 (includes the one-act version of *A View
  from the Bridge*). New York: Library of America, 2006
All My Sons, with commentary and notes by Toby Zinman.
  London: Methuen Drama, 2010
The Crucible, with commentary and notes by Susan C.W.
  Abbotson. London: Methuen Drama, 2010
Death of a Salesman, with commentary and notes by Enoch Brater.
  London: Methuen Drama, 2010
A View from the Bridge (one-act version, with *A Memory of Two
  Mondays*). New York: Viking Press, 1955
A View from the Bridge (two-act version with an introduction by
  Arthur Miller). New York: Penguin, 1977
Echoes Down the Corridor: Collected Essays 1944–2000, ed. Steven R.
  Centola. London: Methuen, 2000
Timebends: A Life. London: Methuen, 1987
'The Family in Modern Drama' in *The Theatre Essays of Arthur
  Miller*, ed. Robert A. Martin. London: Methuen, 1994
'Introduction to the *Collected Plays*' in *The Theatre Essays of Arthur
  Miller*, ed. Robert A. Martin. London: Methuen, 1994

'On Social Plays' in *The Theatre Essays of Arthur Miller*, ed. Robert
A Martin. London: Methuen, 1994
'Tragedy and the Common Man' in *The Theatre Essays of Arthur
Miller*, ed. Robert A Martin. London: Methuen, 1994

Criticism

Abbotson, Susan C. W. *Critical Companion to Arthur Miller*. New
York: Facts on File Inc., 2007
Bigsby, Christopher, *Arthur Miller 1915–1962*. London:
Weidenfeld and Nicolson, 2009
—, *Arthur Miller: A Critical Study*. Cambridge: Cambridge
University Press, 2005
—, *A Critical Introduction to Twentieth-Century American Drama, Vol.
Two: Tennessee Williams, Arthur Miller, Edward Albee*. Cambridge:
Cambridge University Press, 1984
—, *Modern American Drama 1945–1990*. Cambridge: Cambridge
University Press, 1992
Bloom, Harold, ed. *Arthur Miller: Modern Critical Views*. New York:
Chelsea House, 1987
Brater, Enoch. *Arthur Miller: A Playwright's Life and Works*. London:
Thames and Hudson, 2005
—, 'A Dominican *View*: An Interview with Darryl V. Jones' in
Arthur Miller's Global Theater, ed. Enoch Brater. Ann Arbor, MI:
University of Michigan Press, 2007, 87–96
Brater, Enoch, ed. *Arthur Miller's America: Theater and Culture in
Time of Change*. Ann Arbor: University of Michigan Press, 2005
Carson, Neil. '*A View from the Bridge* and the Expansion of Vision'
in *Arthur Miller; Modern Critical Views*, ed. Harold Bloom. New
York: Chelsea House, 1987
Centola, Steven, R. 'Compromise as Bad Faith: Arthur Miller's
A View from the Bridge and William Inge's *Come Back Little Sheba*',
Midwest Quarterly, 28, no. 1 (Autumn 1986), 100–13
—, and Michelle Cirulli. *The Critical Response to Arthur Miller*.
Westport, CT: Praeger, 2006
Costello, Donald P. 'Arthur Miller's Circles of Responsibility:
A View from the Bridge and Beyond'. *Modern Drama*, 36 (1993),
443–53

Epstein, Arthur. 'A Look at *A View from The Bridge*', *Texas Studies in Language and Literature*, 7 (1965), 109–22

Horan, Thomas. 'Another View from the Bridge', *Arthur Miller Journal*, 3, 1 (Spring 2008), 17–28

Hurd, Myles, R. 'Angels and Anxieties in Miller's *A View from the Bridge*', *Notes on Contemporary Literature*, 13 (1983), 4–6

Marino, Stephen A. 'Territoriality in Arthur Miller's *A View from the Bridge*' in *Arthur Miller: Twentieth-Century Legend*, ed. Syed Mashkoor Ali. Jaippur, India: Surabhi, 2006, 203–15

—, 'Verse, Figurative Language and Myth in *A View from the Bridge*' in *A Language Study of Arthur Miller's Plays: The Poetic in the Colloquial*. Lewiston, ME: Edwin Mellen Press, 2002, 81–106

Moss, Leonard. 'Arthur Miller and the Common Man's Language', *Modern Drama*, 7 (1964), 52–9

Rothenberg, Albert, and Eugene D. Shapiro. 'The Defense of Psychoanalysis in Literature: *Long Day's Journey into Night* and *A View from the Bridge*', *Comparative Drama*, 7, 1 (Spring 1973), 51–67. Rpt. in *Critical Approaches to O'Neill*, ed. John H. Stroupe. New York: AMS, 1988, 169–85

Roudané, Matthew C., ed. *Conversations With Arthur Miller*. Jackson, MS: University of Mississippi Press, 1987

Otten, Terry, '*A View from the Bridge*', in *The Temptation of Innocence in the Drama of Arthur Miller*. Columbia, MO: University of Missouri Press, 2002, 76–88

Styan, J. L. 'Why *A View from the Bridge* Went Down Well in London: The Story of a Revision' in *Arthur Miller: New Perspective*, ed. Robert A. Martin. Englewood Cliffs, NJ: Prentice Hall, 1982, 139–48

Wertheim, Albert. '*A View from the Bridge*' in *Cambridge Companion to Arthur Miller*, ed. Christopher Bigsby. Cambridge: Cambridge University Press, 1997

A View from the Bridge

A Play in Two Acts

Characters

Louis
Mike
Alfieri
Eddie
Catherine
Beatrice
Marco
Tony
Rodolpho
First Immigration Officer
Second Immigration Officer
Mr Lipari
Mrs Lipari
Two 'Submarines'
Neighbours

Act One

The street and house front of a tenement building. The front is skeletal entirely. The main acting area is the living room-dining room of **Eddie**'*s apartment. It is a worker's flat, clean, sparse, homely. There is a rocker down front; a round dining table at center, with chairs; and a portable phonograph.*

At back are a bedroom door and an opening to the kitchen; none of these interiors are seen.

At the right, forestage, a desk. This is **Mr Alfieri**'*s law office. There is also a telephone booth. This is not used until the last scenes, so it may be covered or left in view.*

A stairway leads up to the apartment, and then farther up to the next story, which is not seen.

Ramps, representing the street, run upstage and off to right and left.

As the curtain rises, **Louis** *and* **Mike**, *longshoremen, are pitching coins against the building at left.*

A distant foghorn blows.

Enter **Alfieri**, *a lawyer in his fifties turning gray; he is portly, good-humored, and thoughtful. The two pitchers nod to him as he passes. He crosses the stage to his desk, removes his hat, runs his fingers through his hair, and grinning, speaks to the audience.*

Alfieri You wouldn't have known it, but something amusing has just happened. You see how uneasily they nod to me? That's because I am a lawyer. In this neighborhood to meet a lawyer or a priest on the street is unlucky. We're only thought of in connection with disasters, and they'd rather not get too close.

I often think that behind that suspicious little nod of theirs lie three thousand years of distrust. A lawyer means the law, and in Sicily, from where their fathers came, the law has not been a friendly idea since the Greeks were beaten.

I am inclined to notice the ruins in things, perhaps because I was born in Italy . . . I only came here when I was twenty-five.

In those days, Al Capone, the greatest Carthaginian of all, was learning his trade on these pavements, and Frankie Yale himself was cut precisely in half by a machine gun on the corner of Union Street, two blocks away. Oh, there were many here who were justly shot by unjust men. Justice is very important here.

But this is Red Hook, not Sicily. This is the slum that faces the bay on the seaward side of Brooklyn Bridge. This is the gullet of New York swallowing the tonnage of the world. And now we are quite civilized, quite American. Now we settle for half, and I like it better. I no longer keep a pistol in my filing cabinet.

And my practice is entirely unromantic.

My wife has warned me, so have my friends; they tell me the people in this neighborhood lack elegance, glamour. After all, who have I dealt with in my life? Longshoremen and their wives, and fathers and grandfathers, compensation cases, evictions, family squabbles – the petty troubles of the poor – and yet . . . every few years there is still a case, and as the parties tell me what the trouble is, the flat air in my office suddenly washes in with the green scent of the sea, the dust in this air is blown away and the thought comes that in some Caesar's year, in Calabria perhaps or on the cliff at Syracuse, another lawyer, quite differently dressed, heard the same complaint and sat there as powerless as I, and watched it run its bloody course.

Eddie *has appeared and has been pitching coins with the men and is highlighted among them. He is forty – a husky, slightly overweight longshoreman.*

Alfieri   This one's name was Eddie Carbone, a longshoreman working the docks from Brooklyn Bridge to the breakwater where the open sea begins.

Alfieri *walks into darkness.*

Eddie (*moving up steps into doorway*)   Well, I'll see ya, fellas.

Catherine *enters from kitchen, crosses down to window, looks out.*

Louis   You workin' tomorrow?

Eddie   Yeah, there's another day yet on that ship. See ya, Louis.

Eddie *goes into the house, as light rises in the apartment.* **Catherine** *is waving to* **Louis** *from the window and turns to him.*

Catherine   Hi, Eddie!

Eddie *is pleased and therefore shy about it; he hangs up his cap and jacket.*

Eddie   Where you goin' all dressed up?

Catherine (*running her hands over her skirt*)   I just got it. You like it?

Eddie   Yeah, it's nice. And what happened to your hair?

Catherine   You like it? I fixed it different. (*Calling to kitchen.*) He's here, B!

Eddie   Beautiful. Turn around, lemme see in the back. (*She turns for him.*) Oh, if your mother was alive to see you now! She wouldn't believe it.

Catherine   You like it, huh?

Eddie   You look like one of them girls that went to college. Where you goin'?

Catherine (*taking his arm*)   Wait'll B comes in, I'll tell you something. Here, sit down. (*She is walking him to the armchair. Calling offstage.*) Hurry up, will you, B?

Eddie (*sitting*)   What's goin' on?

Catherine   I'll get you a beer, all right?

Eddie   Well, tell me what happened. Come over here, talk to me.

Catherine   I want to wait till B comes in. (*She sits on her heels beside him.*) Guess how much we paid for the skirt.

Eddie   I think it's too short, ain't it?

Catherine (*standing*)   No! not when I stand up.

Eddie   Yeah, but you gotta sit down sometimes.

Catherine   Eddie, it's the style now. (*She walks to show him.*) I mean, if you see me walkin' down the street –

Eddie   Listen, you been givin' me the willies the way you walk down the street, I mean it.

Catherine   Why?

Eddie   Catherine, I don't want to be a pest, but I'm tellin' you you're walkin' wavy.

Catherine   I'm walkin' wavy?

Eddie   Now don't aggravate me, Katie, you are walkin' wavy! I don't like the looks they're givin' you in the candy store. And with them new high heels on the sidewalk – clack, clack, clack. The heads are turnin' like windmills.

Catherine   But those guys look at all the girls, you know that.

Eddie   You ain't 'all the girls'.

Catherine   (*almost in tears because he disapproves*)   What do you want me to do? You want me to –

Eddie   Now don't get mad, kid.

Catherine   Well, I don't know what you want from me.

Eddie   Katie, I promised your mother on her deathbed. I'm responsible for you. You're a baby, you don't understand these things. I mean like when you stand here by the window, wavin' outside.

Catherine   I was wavin' to Louis!

Eddie   Listen, I could tell you things about Louis which you wouldn't wave to him no more.

Catherine   (*trying to joke him out of his warning*)   Eddie, I wish there was one guy you couldn't tell me things about!

Eddie   Catherine, do me a favor, will you? You're gettin' to be a big girl now, you gotta keep yourself more, you can't be so friendly, kid. (*Calls.*) Hey, B, what're you doin' in there? (*To* **Catherine**.) Get her in here, will you? I got news for her.

Catherine (*starting out*)   What?

Eddie   Her cousins landed.

Catherine (*clapping her hands together*)   No! (*She turns instantly and starts for the kitchen.*) B! Your cousins!

Beatrice *enters, wiping her hands with a towel.*

Beatrice (*in the face of* **Catherine**'*s shout*)   What?

Catherine   Your cousins got in!

Beatrice (*astounded, turns to* **Eddie**)   What are you talkin' about? Where?

Eddie   I was just knockin' off work before and Tony Bereli come over to me; he says the ship is in the North River.

Beatrice (*her hands are clasped at her breast; she seems half in fear, half in unutterable joy*)   They're all right?

Eddie   He didn't see them yet, they're still on board. But as soon as they get off he'll meet them. He figures about ten o'clock they'll be here.

Beatrice (*sits, almost weak from tension*)   And they'll let them off the ship all right? That's fixed, heh?

Eddie   Sure, they give them regular seamen papers and they walk off with the crew. Don't worry about it, B, there's nothin' to it. Couple of hours they'll be here.

Beatrice   What happened? They wasn't supposed to be till next Thursday.

Eddie   I don't know; they put them on any ship they can get them out on. Maybe the other ship they was supposed to take there was some danger – What you cryin' about?

Beatrice (*astounded and afraid*)   I'm – I just – I can't believe it! I didn't even buy a new table cloth; I was gonna wash the walls –

Eddie   Listen, they'll think it's a millionaire's house compared to the way they live. Don't worry about the walls. They'll be thankful. (*To* **Catherine**.) Whyn't you run down buy a table cloth. Go ahead, here. (*He is reaching into his pocket.*)

Catherine   There's no stores open now.

Eddie (*to* **Beatrice**)   You was gonna put a new cover on the chair.

Beatrice   I know – well, I thought it was gonna be next week! I was gonna clean the walls, I was gonna wax the floors. (*She stands disturbed.*)

Catherine (*pointing upward*)   Maybe Mrs Dondero upstairs –

Beatrice (*of the table cloth*)   No, hers is worse than this one. (*Suddenly.*) My God, I don't even have nothin' to eat for them! (*She starts for the kitchen.*)

Eddie (*reaching out and grabbing her arm*)   Hey, hey! Take it easy.

Beatrice   No, I'm just nervous, that's all. (*To* **Catherine**.) I'll make the fish.

Eddie   You're savin' their lives, what're you worryin' about the table cloth? They probably didn't see a table cloth in their whole life where they come from.

Beatrice (*looking into his eyes*)   I'm just worried about you, that's all I'm worried.

Eddie   Listen, as long as they know where they're gonna sleep.

Beatrice   I told them in the letters. They're sleepin' on the floor.

Eddie   Beatrice, all I'm worried about is you got such a heart that I'll end up on the floor with you, and they'll be in our bed.

Beatrice   All right, stop it.

Eddie   Because as soon as you see a tired relative, I end up on the floor.

Beatrice   When did you end up on the floor?

Eddie   When your father's house burned down I didn't end up on the floor?

Beatrice   Well, their house burned down!

Eddie   Yeah, but it didn't keep burnin' for two weeks!

Beatrice   All right, look, I'll tell them to go someplace else. (*She starts into the kitchen.*)

Eddie   Now wait a minute. Beatrice! (*She halts. He goes to her.*) I just don't want you bein' pushed around, that's all. You got too big a heart. (*He touches her hand.*) What're you so touchy?

Beatrice   I'm just afraid if it don't turn out good you'll be mad at me.

Eddie   Listen, if everybody keeps his mouth shut, nothin' can happen. They'll pay for their board.

Beatrice   Oh, I told them.

Eddie   Then what the hell. (*Pause. He moves.*) It's an honor, B. I mean it. I was just thinkin' before, comin' home, suppose my father didn't come to this country, and I was starvin' like them over there . . . and I had people in America could keep me a couple of months? The man would be honored to lend me a place to sleep.

Beatrice (*there are tears in her eyes. She turns to* **Catherine**)   You see what he is? (*She turns and grabs* **Eddie**'*s face in her hands.*) Mmm! You're an angel! God'll bless you. (*He is gratefully smiling.*) You'll see, you'll get a blessing for this!

Eddie (*laughing*)   I'll settle for my own bed.

Beatrice   Go, baby, set the table.

Catherine   We didn't tell him about me yet.

Beatrice   Let him eat first, then we'll tell him. Bring everything in. (*She hurries* **Catherine** *out.*)

Eddie (*sitting at the table*)   What's all that about? Where's she goin'?

Beatrice   Noplace. It's very good news, Eddie. I want you to be happy.

Eddie   What's goin' on?

Catherine *enters with plates, forks.*

Beatrice   She's got a job.

Pause. **Eddie** *looks at* **Catherine**, *then back to* **Beatrice**.

Eddie   What job? She's gonna finish school.

Catherine   Eddie, you won't believe it –

Eddie   No – no, you gonna finish school. What kinda job, what do you mean? All of a sudden you –

Catherine   Listen a minute, it's wonderful.

Eddie   It's not wonderful. You'll never get nowheres unless you finish school. You can't take no job. Why didn't you ask me before you take a job?

Beatrice   She's askin' you now, she didn't take nothin' yet.

Catherine   Listen a minute! I came to school this morning and the principal called me out of the class, see? To go to his office.

Eddie   Yeah?

Catherine   So I went in and he says to me he's got my records, y'know? And there's a company wants a girl right away. It ain't exactly a secretary, it's a stenographer first, but pretty soon you get to be secretary. And he says to me that I'm the best student in the whole class –

Beatrice   You hear that?

Eddie   Well why not? Sure she's the best.

Catherine   I'm the best student, he says, and if I want, I should take the job and the end of the year he'll let me take the examination and he'll give me the certificate. So I'll save practically a year!

Eddie (*strangely nervous*)   Where's the job? What company?

Catherine   It's a big plumbing company over Nostrand Avenue.

Eddie   Nostrand Avenue and where?

Catherine   It's someplace by the Navy Yard.

Beatrice   Fifty dollars a week, Eddie.

Eddie (*to* **Catherine**, *surprised*)   Fifty?

Catherine   I swear.

Pause.

Eddie   What about all the stuff you wouldn't learn this year, though?

Catherine   There's nothin' more to learn, Eddie, I just gotta practice from now on. I know all the symbols and I know the keyboard. I'll just get faster, that's all. And when I'm workin' I'll keep gettin' better and better, you see?

Beatrice   Work is the best practice anyway.

Eddie   That ain't what I wanted, though.

Catherine   Why! It's a great big company –

Eddie   I don't like that neighborhood over there.

Catherine   It's a block and half from the subway, he says.

Eddie   Near the Navy Yard plenty can happen in a block and a half. And a plumbin' company! That's one step over the water front. They're practically longshoremen.

Beatrice   Yeah, but she'll be in the office, Eddie.

Eddie   I know she'll be in the office, but that ain't what I had in mind.

Beatrice   Listen, she's gotta go to work sometime.

Eddie   Listen, B, she'll be with a lotta plumbers? And sailors up and down the street? So what did she go to school for?

Catherine   But it's fifty a week, Eddie.

Eddie   Look, did I ask you for money? I supported you this long I support you a little more. Please, do me a favor, will ya? I want you to be with different kind of people. I want you to be in a nice office. Maybe a lawyer's office someplace in New York in one of them nice buildings. I mean if you're gonna get outa here then get out; don't go practically in the same kind of neighborhood.

Pause. **Catherine** *lowers her eyes.*

Beatrice   Go, baby, bring in the supper. (**Catherine** *goes out.*) Think about it a little bit, Eddie. Please. She's crazy to start work. It's not a little shop, it's a big company. Some day she could be a secretary. They picked her out of the whole class. (*He is silent, staring down at the tablecloth, fingering the pattern.*) What are you worried about? She could take care of herself. She'll get out of the subway and be in the office in two minutes.

Eddie (*somehow sickened*)   I know that neighborhood, B, I don't like it.

Beatrice   Listen, if nothin' happened to her in this neighborhood it ain't gonna happen noplace else. (*She turns his face to her.*) Look, you gotta get used to it, she's no baby no more. Tell her to take it. (*He turns his head away.*) You hear me? (*She is angering.*) I don't understand you; she's seventeen years old, you gonna keep her in the house all her life?

Eddie (*insulted*)   What kinda remark is that?

Beatrice (*with sympathy but insistent force*)   Well, I don't understand when it ends. First it was gonna be when she graduated high school, so she graduated high school. Then it was gonna be when she learned stenographer, so she learned stenographer. So what're we gonna wait for now? I mean it, Eddie, sometimes I don't understand you; they picked her out of the whole class, it's an honor for her.

Catherine *enters with food, which she silently sets on the table. After a moment of watching her face,* **Eddie** *breaks into a smile, but it almost seems that tears will form in his eyes.*

Eddie   With your hair that way you look like a madonna, you know that? You're the madonna type. (*She doesn't look at him, but continues ladling out food onto the plates.*) You wanna go to work, heh, Madonna?

Catherine (*softly*)   Yeah.

Eddie (*with a sense of her childhood, her babyhood, and the years*) All right, go to work. (*She looks at him, then rushes and hugs him.*) Hey, hey! Take it easy! (*He holds her face away from him to look at her.*) What're you cryin' about? (*He is affected by her, but smiles his emotion away.*)

Catherine (*sitting at her place*)   I just – (*Bursting out.*) I'm gonna buy all new dishes with my first pay! (*They laugh warmly.*) I mean it. I'll fix up the whole house! I'll buy a rug!

Eddie   And then you'll move away.

Catherine   No, Eddie!

Eddie (*grinning*)   Why not? That's life. And you'll come visit on Sundays, then once a month, then Christmas and New Year's, finally.

Catherine (*grasping his arm to reassure him and to erase the accusation*) No, please!

Eddie (*smiling but hurt*)   I only ask you one thing – don't trust nobody. You got a good aunt but she's got too big a heart, you learned bad from her. Believe me.

Beatrice   Be the way you are, Katie, don't listen to him.

Eddie (*to* **Beatrice** *– strangely and quickly resentful*)   You lived in a house all your life, what do you know about it? You never worked in your life.

Beatrice   She likes people. What's wrong with that?

Eddie   Because most people ain't people. She's goin' to work; plumbers; they'll chew her to pieces if she don't watch out. (*To* **Catherine**.) Believe me, Katie, the less you trust, the less you be sorry.

Eddie *crosses himself and the women do the same, and they eat.*

Catherine   First thing I'll buy is a rug, heh, B?

Beatrice   I don't mind. (*To* **Eddie**.) I smelled coffee all day today. You unloadin' coffee today?

Eddie   Yeah, a Brazil ship.

Catherine   I smelled it too. It smelled all over the neighborhood.

Eddie   That's one time, boy, to be a longshoreman is a pleasure. I could work coffee ships twenty hours a day. You go down in the hold, y'know? It's like flowers, that smell. We'll bust a bag tomorrow, I'll bring you some.

Beatrice   Just be sure there's no spiders in it, will ya? I mean it. (*She directs this to* **Catherine**, *rolling her eyes upward.*) I still remember that spider coming out of that bag he brung home. I nearly died.

Eddie   You call that a spider? You oughta see what comes outa the bananas sometimes.

Beatrice   Don't talk about it!

Eddie   I seen spiders could stop a Buick.

Beatrice (*clapping her hands over her ears*)   All right, shut up!

Eddie (*laughing and taking a watch out of his pocket*)   Well, who started with spiders?

Beatrice   All right, I'm sorry, I didn't mean it. Just don't bring none home again. What time is it?

Eddie   Quarter nine. (*Puts watch back in his pocket.*)

They continue eating in silence.

Catherine   He's bringin' them ten o'clock, Tony?

Eddie   Around, yeah. (*He eats.*)

Catherine   Eddie, suppose somebody asks if they're livin' here. (*He looks at her as though already she had divulged something publicly. Defensively.*) I mean if they ask.

Eddie   Now look, baby, I can see we're gettin' mixed up again here.

Catherine   No, I just mean . . . people'll see them goin' in and out.

Eddie   I don't care who sees them goin' in and out as long as you don't see them goin' in and out. And this goes for you too, B. You don't see nothin' and you don't know nothin'.

Beatrice   What do you mean? I understand.

Eddie   You don't understand; you still think you can talk about this to somebody just a little bit. Now lemme say it once and for all, because you're makin' me nervous again, both of you. I don't care if somebody comes in the house and sees them sleepin' on the floor, it never comes out of your mouth who they are or what they're doin' here.

Beatrice   Yeah, but my mother'll know –

Eddie   Sure she'll know, but just don't you be the one who told her, that's all. This is the United States government you're playin' with now, this is the Immigration Bureau. If you said it you knew it, if you didn't say it you didn't know it.

Catherine   Yeah, but Eddie, suppose somebody –

Eddie   I don't care what question it is. You – don't – know – nothin'. They got stool pigeons all over this neighborhood they're payin' them every week for information, and you don't know who they are. It could be your best friend. You hear? (*To* **Beatrice**.) Like Vinny Bolzano, remember Vinny?

Beatrice   Oh, yeah. God forbid.

Eddie   Tell her about Vinny. (*To* **Catherine**.) You think I'm blowin' steam here? (*To* **Beatrice**.) Go ahead, tell her. (*To*

Catherine.) You was a baby then. There was a family lived next door to her mother, he was about sixteen –

Beatrice   No, he was no more than fourteen, 'cause I was to his confirmation in Saint Agnes. But the family had an uncle that they were hidin' in the house, and he snitched to the Immigration.

Catherine   The kid snitched?

Eddie   On his own uncle!

Catherine   What, was he crazy?

Eddie   He was crazy after, I tell you that, boy.

Beatrice   Oh, it was terrible. He had five brothers and the old father. And they grabbed him in the kitchen and pulled him down the stairs – three flights his head was bouncin' like a coconut. And they spit on him in the street, his own father and his brothers. The whole neighborhood was cryin'.

Catherine   Ts! So what happened to him?

Beatrice   I think he went away. (*To* **Eddie**.) I never seen him again, did you?

Eddie (*rises during this, taking out his watch*)   Him? You'll never see him no more, a guy do a thing like that? How's he gonna show his face? (*To* **Catherine**, *as he gets up uneasily.*) Just remember, kid, you can quicker get back a million dollars that was stole than a word that you gave away. (*He is standing now, stretching his back.*)

Catherine   Okay, I won't say a word to nobody, I swear.

Eddie   Gonna rain tomorrow. We'll be slidin' all over the decks. Maybe you oughta put something on for them, they be here soon.

Beatrice   I only got fish, I hate to spoil it if they ate already. I'll wait, it only takes a few minutes; I could broil it.

Catherine   What happens, Eddie, when that ship pulls out and they ain't on it, though? Don't the captain say nothin'?

Eddie (*slicing an apple with his pocket knife*)   Captain's pieced off, what do you mean?

Catherine   Even the captain?

Eddie   What's the matter, the captain don't have to live? Captain gets a piece, maybe one of the mates, piece for the guy in Italy who fixed the papers for them, Tony here'll get a little bite . . .

Beatrice   I just hope they get work here, that's all I hope.

Eddie   Oh, the Syndicate'll fix jobs for them; till they pay 'em off they'll get them work every day. It's after the pay-off, then they'll have to scramble like the rest of us.

Beatrice   Well, it be better than they got there.

Eddie   Oh sure, well, listen. So you gonna start Monday, heh, Madonna?

Catherine (*embarrassed*)   I'm supposed to, yeah.

Eddie *is standing facing the two seated women. First* **Beatrice** *smiles, then* **Catherine**, *for a powerful emotion is on him, a childish one and a knowing fear, and the tears show in his eyes – and they are shy before the avowal.*

Eddie (*sadly smiling, yet somehow proud of her*)   Well . . . I hope you have good luck. I wish you the best. You know that, kid.

Catherine (*rising, trying to laugh*)   You sound like I'm goin' a million miles!

Eddie   I know. I guess I just never figured on one thing.

Catherine (*smiling*)   What?

Eddie   That you would ever grow up. (*He utters a soundless laugh at himself, feeling his breast pocket of his shirt.*) I left a cigar in my other coat, I think. (*He starts for the bedroom.*)

Catherine   Stay there! I'll get it for you.

She hurries out. There is a slight pause, and **Eddie** *turns to* **Beatrice**, *who has been avoiding his gaze.*

Eddie   What are you mad at me lately?

Beatrice   Who's mad? (*She gets up, clearing the dishes.*) I'm not mad. (*She picks up the dishes and turns to him.*) You're the one is mad. (*She turns and goes into the kitchen as* **Catherine** *enters from the bedroom with a cigar and a pack of matches.*)

Catherine   Here! I'll light it for you! (*She strikes a match and holds it to his cigar. He puffs. Quietly.*) Don't worry about me, Eddie, heh?

Eddie   Don't burn yourself. (*Just in time she blows out the match.*) You better go in help her with the dishes.

Catherine (*turns quickly to the table, and, seeing the table cleared, she says, almost guiltily*)   Oh! (*She hurries into the kitchen, and as she exits there.*) I'll do the dishes, B!

Alone, **Eddie** *stands looking toward the kitchen for a moment. Then he takes out his watch, glances at it, replaces it in his pocket, sits in the armchair, and stares at the smoke flowing out of his mouth.*

The lights go down, then come up on **Alfieri**, *who has moved onto the forestage.*

Alfieri   He was as good a man as he had to be in a life that was hard and even. He worked on the piers when there was work, he brought home his pay, and he lived. And toward ten o'clock of that night, after they had eaten, the cousins came.

The lights fade on **Alfieri** *and rise on the street.*

Enter **Tony**, *escorting* **Marco** *and* **Rodolpho**, *each with a valise.* **Tony** *halts, indicates the house. They stand for a moment looking at it.*

Marco (*he is a square-built peasant of thirty-two, suspicious, tender, and quiet-voiced*)   Thank you.

Tony   You're on your own now. Just be careful, that's all. Ground floor.

Marco   Thank you.

Tony (*indicating the house*)   I'll see you on the pier tomorrow. You'll go to work.

Marco *nods.* **Tony** *continues on walking down the street.*

Rodolpho   This will be the first house I ever walked into in America! Imagine! She said they were poor!

Marco   Ssh! Come. (*They go to door.*)

Marco *knocks. The lights rise in the room.* **Eddie** *goes and opens the door. Enter* **Marco** *and* **Rodolpho**, *removing their caps.* **Beatrice** *and* **Catherine** *enter from the kitchen. The lights fade in the street.*

Eddie   You Marco?

Marco   Marco.

Eddie   Come on in! (*He shakes* **Marco***'s hand.*)

Beatrice   Here, take the bags!

Marco (*nods, looks to the women and fixes on* **Beatrice**. *Crosses to* **Beatrice**)   Are you my cousin?

She nods. He kisses her hand.

Beatrice (*above the table, touching her chest with her hand*)   Beatrice. This is my husband, Eddie. (*All nod.*) Catherine, my sister Nancy's daughter. (*The brothers nod.*)

Marco (*indicating* **Rodolpho**)   My brother. Rodolpho. (**Rodolpho** *nods.* **Marco** *comes with a certain formal stiffness to* **Eddie**.) I want to tell you now, Eddie – when you say go, we will go.

Eddie   Oh, no . . . (*Takes* **Marco***'s bag.*)

Marco   I see it's a small house, but soon, maybe, we can have our own house.

Eddie   You're welcome, Marco, we got plenty of room here. Katie, give them supper, heh? (*Exits into bedroom with their bags.*)

Catherine   Come here, sit down. I'll get you some soup.

Marco (*as they go to the table*)   We ate on the ship. Thank you. (*To* **Eddie**, *calling off to bedroom.*) Thank you.

Beatrice   Get some coffee. We'll all have coffee. Come sit down.

Rodolpho *and* **Marco** *sit, at the table.*

Catherine (*wondrously*)   How come he's so dark and you're so light, Rodolpho?

Rodolpho (*ready to laugh*)   I don't know. A thousand years ago, they say, the Danes invaded Sicily.

Beatrice *kisses* **Rodolpho**. *They laugh as* **Eddie** *enters.*

Catherine (*to* **Beatrice**)   He's practically blond!

Eddie   How's the coffee doin'?

Catherine (*brought up*)   I'm gettin' it. (*She hurries out to kitchen.*)

Eddie (*sits on his rocker*)   Yiz have a nice trip?

Marco   The ocean is always rough. But we are good sailors.

Eddie   No trouble gettin' here?

Marco   No. The man brought us. Very nice man.

Rodolpho (*to* **Eddie**)   He says we start to work tomorrow. Is he honest?

Eddie (*laughing*)   No. But as long as you owe them money, they'll get you plenty of work. (*To* **Marco**.) Yiz ever work on the piers in Italy?

Marco   Piers? Ts! – no.

Rodolpho (*smiling at the smallness of his town*)   In our town there are no piers, only the beach, and little fishing boats.

Beatrice   So what kinda work did yiz do?

Marco (*shrugging shyly, even embarrassed*)   Whatever there is, anything.

Rodolpho   Sometimes they build a house, or if they fix the bridge – Marco is a mason and I bring him the cement. (*He laughs.*) In harvest time we work in the fields . . . if there is work. Anything.

Eddie   Still bad there, heh?

Marco   Bad, yes.

Rodolpho (*laughing*)   It's terrible! We stand around all day in the piazza listening to the fountain like birds. Everybody waits only for the train.

Beatrice   What's on the train?

Rodolpho   Nothing. But if there are many passengers and you're lucky you make a few lire to push the taxi up the hill.

Enter **Catherine***; she listens.*

Beatrice   You gotta push a taxi?

Rodolpho (*laughing*)   Oh, sure! It's a feature in our town. The horses in our town are skinnier than goats. So if there are too many passengers we help to push the carriages up to the hotel. (*He laughs.*) In our town the horses are only for show.

Catherine   Why don't they have automobile taxis?

Rodolpho   There is one. We push that too. (*They laugh.*) Everything in our town, you gotta push!

Beatrice (*to* **Eddie**)   How do you like that!

Eddie (*to* **Marco**)   So what're you wanna do, you gonna stay here in this country or you wanna go back?

Marco (*surprised*)   Go back?

Eddie   Well, you're married, ain't you?

Marco   Yes. I have three children.

Beatrice   Three! I thought only one.

Marco   Oh, no. I have three now. Four years, five years, six years.

Beatrice   Ah . . . I bet they're cryin' for you already, heh?

Marco   What can I do? The older one is sick in his chest. My wife – she feeds them from her own mouth. I tell you the truth, if I stay there they will never grow up. They eat the sunshine.

Beatrice   My God. So how long you want to stay?

Marco   With your permission, we will stay maybe a –

Eddie   She don't mean in this house, she means in the country.

Marco   Oh. Maybe four, five, six years, I think.

Rodolpho (*smiling*)   He trusts his wife.

Beatrice   Yeah, but maybe you'll get enough, you'll be able to go back quicker.

Marco   I hope. I don't know. (*To* **Eddie**.) I understand it's not so good here either.

Eddie   Oh, you guys'll be all right – till you pay them off, anyway. After that, you'll have to scramble, that's all. But you'll make better here than you could there.

Rodolpho   How much? We hear all kinds of figures. How much can a man make? We work hard, we'll work all day, all night –

Marco *raises a hand to hush him.*

Eddie (*he is coming more and more to address* **Marco** *only*)   On the average a whole year? Maybe – well, it's hard to say, see. Sometimes we lay off, there's no ships three four weeks.

Marco   Three, four weeks! – Ts!

Eddie   But I think you could probably – thirty, forty a week, over the whole twelve months of the year.

Marco (*rises, crosses to* **Eddie**)   Dollars.

Eddie   Sure dollars.

Marco *puts an arm round* **Rodolpho** *and they laugh.*

Marco   If we can stay here a few months, Beatrice –

Beatrice   Listen, you're welcome, Marco –

Marco   Because I could send them a little more if I stay here.

Beatrice   As long as you want, we got plenty a room.

Marco (*his eyes are showing tears*)   My wife – (*To* **Eddie**.) My wife – I want to send right away maybe twenty dollars –

Eddie   You could send them something next week already.

Marco (*he is near tears*)   Eduardo . . . (*He goes to* **Eddie**, *offering his hand.*)

Eddie   Don't thank me. Listen, what the hell, it's no skin off me. (*To* **Catherine**.) What happened to the coffee?

Catherine   I got it on. (*To* **Rodolpho**.) You married too? No.

Rodolpho (*rises*)   Oh, no . . .

Beatrice (*to* **Catherine**)   I told you he –

Catherine   I know, I just thought maybe he got married recently.

Rodolpho   I have no money to get married. I have a nice face, but no money. (*He laughs.*)

Catherine (*to* **Beatrice**)   He's a real blond!

Beatrice (*to* **Rodolpho**)   You want to stay here too, heh? For good?

Rodolpho   Me? Yes, for ever! Me, I want to be an American. And then I want to go back to Italy when I am rich, and I will buy a motorcycle. (*He smiles.* **Marco** *shakes him affectionately.*)

Catherine   A motorcycle!

Rodolpho   With a motorcycle in Italy you will never starve any more.

Beatrice   I'll get you coffee. (*She exits to the kitchen.*)

Eddie   What you do with a motorcycle?

Marco   He dreams, he dreams.

Rodolpho (*to* **Marco**)   Why? (*To* **Eddie**.) Messages! The rich people in the hotel always need someone who will carry a message. But quickly, and with a great noise. With a blue motorcycle I would station myself in the courtyard of the hotel, and in a little while I would have messages.

Marco   When you have no wife you have dreams.

Eddie   Why can't you just walk, or take a trolley or sump'm?

Enter **Beatrice** *with coffee.*

Rodolpho   Oh, no, the machine, the machine is necessary. A man comes into a great hotel and says, I am a messenger. Who is this man? He disappears walking, there is no noise, nothing. Maybe he will never come back, maybe he will never deliver the message. But a man who rides up on a great machine, this man is responsible, this man exists. He will be given messages. (*He helps* **Beatrice** *set out the coffee things.*) I am also a singer, though.

Eddie   You mean a regular – ?

Rodolpho   Oh, yes. One night last year Andreola got sick. Baritone. And I took his place in the garden of the hotel. Three arias I sang without a mistake! Thousand-lire notes they threw from the tables, money was falling like a storm in the treasury. It was magnificent. We lived six months on that night, eh, Marco?

Marco *nods doubtfully.*

Marco   Two months.

Eddie *laughs.*

Beatrice   Can't you get a job in that place?

Rodolpho   Andreola got better. He's a baritone, very strong.

Beatrice *laughs.*

Marco (*regretfully, to* **Beatrice**)   He sang too loud.

Rodolpho   Why too loud?

Marco   Too loud. The guests in that hotel are all Englishmen. They don't like too loud.

Rodolpho (*to* **Catherine**)   Nobody ever said it was too loud!

Marco   I say. It was too loud. (*To* **Beatrice**.) I knew it as soon as he started to sing. Too loud.

Rodolpho   Then why did they throw so much money?

Marco   They paid for your courage. The English like courage. But once is enough.

Rodolpho (*to all but* **Marco**)   I never heard anybody say it was too loud.

Catherine   Did you ever hear of jazz?

Rodolpho   Oh, sure! I *sing* jazz.

Catherine (*rises*)   You could sing jazz?

Rodolpho   Oh, I sing Napolidan, jazz, bel canto – I sing 'Paper Doll', you like 'Paper Doll'?

Catherine   Oh, sure, I'm crazy for 'Paper Doll'. Go ahead, sing it.

Rodolpho (*takes his stance after getting a nod of permission from* **Marco**, *and with a high tenor voice begins singing*)
    'I'll tell you boys it's tough to be alone,
    And it's tough to love a doll that's not your own.
    I'm through with all of them,
    I'll never fall again,
    Hey, boy, what you gonna do?
    I'm gonna buy a paper doll that I can call my own,
    A doll that other fellows cannot steal.'

Eddie *rises and moves upstage.*

Rodolpho
    'And then those flirty, flirty guys
    With their flirty, flirty eyes
    Will have to flirt with dollies that are real – '

Eddie   Hey, kid – hey, wait a minute –

Catherine (*enthralled*) Leave him finish, it's beautiful! (*To* **Beatrice**.) He's terrific! It's terrific, Rodolpho.

Eddie Look, kid; you don't want to be picked up, do ya?

Marco No – no! (*He rises.*)

Eddie (*indicating the rest of the building*) Because we never had no singers here . . . and all of a sudden there's a singer in the house, y'know what I mean?

Marco Yes, yes. You'll be quiet, Rodolpho.

Eddie (*he is flushed*) They got guys all over the place, Marco. I mean.

Marco Yes. He'll be quiet. (*To* **Rodolpho**.) You'll be quiet.

Rodolpho *nods.*

Eddie *has risen, with iron control, even a smile. He moves to* **Catherine**.

Eddie What's the high heels for, Garbo?

Catherine I figured for tonight –

Eddie Do me a favor, will you? Go ahead.

Embarrassed now, angered, **Catherine** *goes out into the bedroom.* **Beatrice** *watches her go and gets up; in passing, she gives* **Eddie** *a cold look, restrained only by the strangers, and goes to the table to pour coffee.*

Eddie (*striving to laugh, and to* **Marco**, *but directed as much to* **Beatrice**) All actresses they want to be around here.

Rodolpho (*happy about it*) In Italy too! All the girls.

Catherine *emerges from the bedroom in low-heel shoes, comes to the table.* **Rodolpho** *is lifting a cup.*

Eddie (*he is sizing up* **Rodolpho**, *and there is a concealed suspicion*) Yeah, hch?

Rodolpho Yes! (*Laughs, indicating* **Catherine**.) Especially when they are so beautiful!

Catherine You like sugar?

Rodolpho   Sugar? Yes! I like sugar very much!

Eddie *is downstage, watching as she pours a spoonful of sugar into his cup, his face puffed with trouble, and the room dies.*

Lights rise on **Alfieri**.

Alfieri   Who can ever know what will be discovered? Eddie Carbone had never expected to have a destiny. A man works, raises his family, goes bowling, eats, gets old, and then he dies. Now, as the weeks passed, there was a future, there was a trouble that would not go away.

The lights fade on **Alfieri**, *then rise on* **Eddie** *standing at the doorway of the house.* **Beatrice** *enters on the street. She sees* **Eddie**, *smiles at him. He looks away.*

She starts to enter the house when **Eddie** *speaks.*

Eddie   It's after eight.

Beatrice   Well, it's a long show at the Paramount.

Eddie   They must've seen every picture in Brooklyn by now. He's supposed to stay in the house when he ain't working. He ain't supposed to go advertising himself.

Beatrice   Well, that's his trouble, what do you care? If they pick him up they pick him up, that's all. Come in the house.

Eddie   What happened to the stenography? I don't see her practice no more.

Beatrice   She'll get back to it. She's excited, Eddie.

Eddie   She tell you anything?

Beatrice (*comes to him, now the subject is opened*)   What's the matter with you? He's a nice kid, what do you want from him?

Eddie   That's a nice kid? He gives me the heeby-jeebies.

Beatrice (*smiling*)   Ah, go on, you're just jealous.

Eddie   Of *him*? Boy, you don't think much of me.

Beatrice   I don't understand you. What's so terrible about him?

Eddie   You mean it's all right with you? That's gonna be her husband?

Beatrice   Why? He's a nice fella, hard workin', he's a good-lookin' fella.

Eddie   He sings on the ships, didja know that?

Beatrice   What do you mean, he sings?

Eddie   Just what I said, he sings. Right on the deck, all of a sudden, a whole song comes out of his mouth – with motions. You know what they're callin' him now? Paper Doll they're callin' him, Canary. He's like a weird. He comes out on the pier, one-two-three, it's a regular free show.

Beatrice   Well, he's a kid; he don't know how to behave himself yet.

Eddie   And with that wacky hair; he's like a chorus girl or sump'm.

Beatrice   So he's blond, so –

Eddie   I just hope that's his regular hair, that's all I hope.

Beatrice   You crazy or sump'm? (*She tries to turn him to her.*)

Eddie (*he keeps his head turned away*)   What's so crazy? I don't like his whole way.

Beatrice   Listen, you never seen a blond guy in your life? What about Whitey Balsa?

Eddie (*turning to her victoriously*)   Sure, but Whitey don't sing; he don't do like that on the ships.

Beatrice   Well, maybe that's the way they do in Italy.

Eddie   Then why don't his brother sing? Marco goes around like a man; nobody kids Marco. (*He moves from her, halts. She realizes there is a campaign solidified in him.*) I tell you the truth I'm surprised I have to tell you all this. I mean I'm surprised, B.

Beatrice (*she goes to him with purpose now*)   Listen, you ain't gonna start nothin' here.

Eddie   I ain't startin' nothin', but I ain't gonna stand around lookin' at that. For that character I didn't bring her up. I swear, B, I'm surprised at you; I sit there waitin' for you to wake up but everything is great with you.

Beatrice   No, everything ain't great with me.

Eddie   No?

Beatrice   No. But I got other worries.

Eddie   Yeah. (*He is already weakening.*)

Beatrice   Yeah, you want me to tell you?

Eddie (*in retreat*)   Why? What worries you got?

Beatrice   When am I gonna be a wife again, Eddie?

Eddie   I ain't been feelin' good. They bother me since they came.

Beatrice   It's almost three months you don't feel good; they're only here a couple of weeks. It's three months, Eddie.

Eddie   I don't know, B. I don't want to talk about it.

Beatrice   What's the matter, Eddie, you don't like me, heh?

Eddie   What do you mean, I don't like you? I said I don't feel good, that's all.

Beatrice   Well, tell me, am I doing something wrong? Talk to me.

Eddie (*pause. He can't speak, then*)   I can't. I can't talk about it.

Beatrice   Well tell me what –

Eddie   I got nothin' to say about it!

She stands for a moment; he is looking off; she turns to go into the house.

I'll be all right, B; just lay off me, will ya? I'm worried about her.

Beatrice   The girl is gonna be eighteen years old, it's time already.

Eddie   B, he's taking her for a ride!

Beatrice   All right, that's her ride. What're you gonna stand over her till she's forty? Eddie, I want you to cut it out now, you hear me? I don't like it! Now come in the house.

Eddie   I want to take a walk, I'll be in right away.

Beatrice   They ain't goin' to come any quicker if you stand in the street. It ain't nice, Eddie.

Eddie   I'll be in right away. Go ahead. (*He walks off.*)

She goes into the house. **Eddie** *glances up the street, sees* **Louis** *and* **Mike** *coming, and sits on an iron railing.* **Louis** *and* **Mike** *enter.*

Louis   Wanna go bowlin' tonight?

Eddie   I'm too tired. Goin' to sleep.

Louis   How's your two submarines?

Eddie   They're okay.

Louis   I see they're gettin' work allatime.

Eddie   Oh yeah, they're doin' all right.

Mike   That's what we oughta do. We oughta leave the country and come in under the water. Then we get work.

Eddie   You ain't kiddin'.

Louis   Well, what the hell. Y'know?

Eddie   Sure.

Louis (*sits on railing beside* **Eddie**)   Believe me, Eddie, you got a lotta credit comin' to you.

Eddie   Aah, they don't bother me, don't cost me nutt'n.

Mike   That older one, boy, he's a regular bull. I seen him the other day liftin' coffee bags over the Matson Line. They leave him alone he woulda load the whole ship by himself.

Eddie   Yeah, he's a strong guy, that guy. Their father was a regular giant, supposed to be.

Louis   Yeah, you could see. He's a regular slave.

Mike (*grinning*)   That blond one, though – (**Eddie** *looks at him.*) He's got a sense of humor. (**Louis** *snickers.*)

Eddie (*searchingly*)   Yeah. He's funny –

Mike (*starting to laugh*)   Well he ain't exackly funny, but he's always like makin' remarks like, y'know? He comes around, everybody's laughin'. (**Louis** *laughs.*)

Eddie (*uncomfortably, grinning*)   Yeah, well . . . he's got a sense of humor.

Mike (*laughing*)   Yeah, I mean, he's always makin' like remarks, like, y'know?

Eddie   Yeah, I know. But he's a kid yet, y'know? He – he's just a kid, that's all.

Mike (*getting hysterical with* **Louis**)   I know. You take one look at him – everybody's happy. (**Louis** *laughs.*) I worked one day with him last week over the Moore-MacCormack Line, I'm tellin' you they was all hysterical. (**Louis** *and he explode in laughter.*)

Eddie   Why? What'd he do?

Mike   I don't know . . . he was just humorous. You never can remember what he says, y'know? But it's the way he says it. I mean he gives you a look sometimes and you start laughin'!

Eddie   Yeah. (*Troubled.*) He's got a sense of humor.

Mike (*gasping*)   Yeah.

Louis (*rising*)   Well, we see ya, Eddie.

Eddie   Take it easy.

Louis   Yeah. See ya.

Mike   If you wanna come bowlin' later we're goin' Flatbush Avenue.

Laughing, they move to exit, meeting **Rodolpho** *and* **Catherine** *entering on the street. Their laughter rises as they see* **Rodolpho**, *who* *does not understand but joins in.* **Eddie** *moves to enter the house as* **Louis** *and* **Mike** *exit.* **Catherine** *stops him at the door.*

Catherine   Hey, Eddie – what a picture we saw! Did we laugh!

Eddie (*he can't help smiling at sight of her*)   Where'd you go?

Catherine   Paramount. It was with those two guys, y'know? That –

Eddie   Brooklyn Paramount?

Catherine (*with an edge of anger, embarrassed before* **Rodolpho**) Sure, the Brooklyn Paramount. I told you we wasn't goin' to New York.

Eddie (*retreating before the threat of her anger*)   All right, I only asked you. (*To* **Rodolpho**.) I just don't want her hangin' around Times Square, see? It's full of tramps over there.

Rodolpho   I would like to go to Broadway once, Eddie. I would like to walk with her once where the theaters are and the opera. Since I was a boy I see pictures of those lights.

Eddie (*his little patience waning*)   I want to talk to her a minute, Rodolpho. Go inside, will you?

Rodolpho   Eddie, we only walk together in the streets. She teaches me.

Catherine   You know what he can't get over? That there's no fountains in Brooklyn!

Eddie (*smiling unwillingly*)   Fountains? (**Rodolpho** *smiles at his own naivety.*)

Catherine   In Italy he says, every town's got fountains, and they meet there. And you know what? They got oranges on the trees where he comes from, and lemons. Imagine – on the trees? I mean it's interesting. But he's crazy for New York.

Rodolpho (*attempting familiarity*)   Eddie, why can't we go once to Broadway – ?

Eddie   Look, I gotta tell her something –

Rodolpho   Maybe you can come too. I want to see all those lights. (*He sees no response in* **Eddie**'s *face. He glances at* **Catherine**.) I'll walk by the river before I go to sleep. (*He walks off down the street.*)

Catherine   Why don't you talk to him, Eddie? He blesses you, and you don't talk to him hardly.

Eddie (*enveloping her with his eyes*)   I bless you and you don't talk to me. (*He tries to smile.*)

Catherine   *I* don't talk to you? (*She hits his arm.*) What do you mean?

Eddie   I don't see you no more. I come home you're runnin' around someplace –

Catherine   Well, he wants to see everything, that's all, so we go . . . You mad at me?

Eddie   No. (*He moves from her, smiling sadly.*) It's just I used to come home, you was always there. Now, I turn around, you're a big girl. I don't know how to talk to you.

Catherine   Why?

Eddie   I don't know, you're runnin', you're runnin', Katie. I don't think you listening any more to me.

Catherine (*going to him*)   Ah, Eddie, sure I am. What's the matter? You don't like him?

Slight pause.

Eddie (*turns to her*)   *You* like him, Katie?

Catherine (*with a blush but holding her ground*)   Yeah. I like him.

Eddie (*his smile goes*)   You like him.

Catherine (*looking down*)   Yeah. (*Now she looks at him for the consequences, smiling but tense. He looks at her like a lost boy.*) What're you got against him? I don't understand. He only blesses you.

Eddie (*turns away*)   He don't bless me, Katie.

Catherine   He does! You're like a father to him!

Eddie (*turns to her*)   Katie.

Catherine   What, Eddie?

Eddie   You gonna marry him?

Catherine   I don't know. We just been . . . goin' around, that's all. (*Turns to him.*) What're you got against him, Eddie? Please, tell me. What?

Eddie   He don't respect you.

Catherine   Why?

Eddie   Katie . . . if you wasn't an orphan, wouldn't he ask your father's permission before he run around with you like this?

Catherine   Oh, well, he didn't think you'd mind.

Eddie   He knows I mind, but it don't bother him if I mind, don't you see that?

Catherine   No, Eddie, he's got all kinds of respect for me. And you too! We walk across the street he takes my arm – he almost bows to me! You got him all wrong, Eddie; I mean it, you –

Eddie   Katie, he's only bowin' to his passport.

Catherine   His passport!

Eddie   That's right. He marries you he's got the right to be an American citizen. That's what's goin' on here. (*She is puzzled and surprised.*) You understand what I'm tellin' you? The guy is lookin' for his break, that's all he's lookin' for.

Catherine (*pained*)   Oh, no, Eddie, I don't think so.

Eddie   You don't think so! Katie, you're gonna make me cry here. Is that a workin' man? What does he do with his first money? A snappy new jacket he buys, records, a pointy pair new shoes and his brother's kids are starvin' over there with tuberculosis? That's a hit-and-run guy, baby; he's got bright lights in his head, Broadway. Them guys don't think of nobody but theirself! You marry him and the next time you see him it'll be for divorce!

Catherine (*steps toward him*)   Eddie, he never said a word about his papers or –

Eddie   You mean he's supposed to tell you that?

Catherine   I don't think he's even thinking about it.

Eddie   What's better for him to think about! He could be picked up any day here and he's back pushin' taxis up the hill!

Catherine   No, I don't believe it.

Eddie   Katie, don't break my heart, listen to me.

Catherine   I don't want to hear it.

Eddie   Katie, listen . . .

Catherine   He loves me!

Eddie (*with deep alarm*)   Don't say that, for God's sake! This is the oldest racket in the country –

Catherine (*desperately, as though he had made his imprint*)   I don't believe it! (*She rushes to the house.*)

Eddie (*following her*)   They been pullin' this since the Immigration Law was put in! They grab a green kid that don't know nothin' and they –

Catherine (*sobbing*)   I don't believe it and I wish to hell you'd stop it!

Eddie   Katie!

They enter the apartment. The lights in the living room have risen and **Beatrice** *is there. She looks past the sobbing* **Catherine** *at* **Eddie**, *who in the presence of his wife, makes an awkward gesture of eroded command, indicating* **Catherine**.

Eddie   Why don't you straighten her out?

Beatrice (*inwardly angered at his flowing emotion, which in itself alarms her*)   When are you going to leave her alone?

Eddie   B, the guy is no good!

Beatrice (*suddenly, with open fright and fury*)   You going to leave her alone? Or you gonna drive me crazy? (*He turns, striving to retain his dignity, but nevertheless in guilt walks out of the house, into the street and away.* **Catherine** *starts into a bedroom.*) Listen, Catherine. (**Catherine** *halts, turns to her sheepishly.*) What are you going to do with yourself?

Catherine   I don't know.

Beatrice   Don't tell me you don't know; you're not a baby any more, what are you going to do with yourself?

Catherine   He won't listen to me.

Beatrice   I don't understand this. He's not your father, Catherine. I don't understand what's going on here.

Catherine (*as one who herself is trying to rationalize a buried impulse*) What am I going to do, just kick him in the face with it?

Beatrice   Look, honey, you wanna get married, or don't you wanna get married? What are you worried about, Katie?

Catherine (*quietly, trembling*)   I don't know, B. It just seems wrong if he's against it so much.

Beatrice (*never losing her aroused alarm*)   Sit down, honey, I want to tell you something. Here, sit down. Was there ever any fella he liked for you? There wasn't, was there?

Catherine   But he says Rodolpho's just after his papers.

Beatrice   Look, he'll say anything. What does he care what he says? If it was a prince came here for you it would be no different. You know that, don't you?

Catherine   Yeah, I guess.

Beatrice   So what does that mean?

Catherine (*slowly turns her head to* **Beatrice**)   What?

Beatrice   It means you gotta be your own self more. You still think you're a little girl, honey. But nobody else can make up your mind for you any more, you understand? You gotta give him to understand that he can't give you orders no more.

Catherine Yeah, but how am I going to do that? He thinks I'm a baby.

Beatrice Because *you* think you're a baby. I told you fifty times already, you can't act the way you act. You still walk around in front of him in your slip –

Catherine Well I forgot.

Beatrice Well you can't do it. Or like you sit on the edge of the bathtub talkin' to him when he's shavin' in his underwear.

Catherine When'd I do that?

Beatrice I seen you in there this morning.

Catherine Oh . . . well, I wanted to tell him something and I –

Beatrice I know, honey. But if you act like a baby and he be treatin' you like a baby. Like when he comes home sometimes you throw yourself at him like when you was twelve years old.

Catherine Well I like to see him and I'm happy so I –

Beatrice Look, I'm not tellin' you what to do, honey, but –

Catherine No, you could tell me, B! Gee, I'm all mixed up. See, I – He looks so sad now and it hurts me.

Beatrice Well look Katie, if it's goin' to hurt you so much you're gonna end up an old maid here.

Catherine No!

Beatrice I'm tellin' you, I'm not makin' a joke. I tried to tell you a couple of times in the last year or so. That's why I was so happy you were going to go out and get work, you wouldn't be here so much, you'd be a little more independent. I mean it. It's wonderful for a whole family to love each other, but you're a grown woman and you're in the same house with a grown man. So you'll act different now, heh?

Catherine   Yeah, I will. I'll remember.

Beatrice   Because it ain't only up to him, Katie, you understand? I told him the same thing already.

Catherine (*quickly*)   What?

Beatrice   That he should let you go. But, you see, if only I tell him, he thinks I'm just bawlin' him out, or maybe I'm jealous or somethin', you know?

Catherine (*astonished*)   He said you was jealous?

Beatrice   No, I'm just sayin' maybe that's what he thinks. (*She reaches over to* **Catherine**'s *hand; with a strained smile.*) You think I'm jealous of you, honey?

Catherine   No! It's the first I thought of it.

Beatrice (*with a quiet sad laugh*)   Well you should have thought of it before . . . but I'm not. We'll be all right. Just give him to understand; you don't have to fight, you're just – You're a woman, that's all, and you got a nice boy, and now the time came when you said goodbye. All right?

Catherine (*strangely moved at the prospect*)   All right . . . If I can.

Beatrice   Honey . . . you gotta.

Catherine, *sensing now an imperious demand, turns with some fear, with a discovery, to* **Beatrice**. *She is at the edge of tears, as though a familiar world had shattered.*

Catherine   Okay.

Lights out on them and up on **Alfieri**, *seated behind his desk.*

Alfieri   It was at this time that he first came to me. I had represented his father in an accident case some years before, and I was acquainted with the family in a casual way. I remember him now as he walked through my doorway –

Enter **Eddie** *down right ramp.*

Alfieri   His eyes were like tunnels; my first thought was that he had committed a crime –

Eddie *sits besides the desk, cap in hand, looking out.*

Alfieri   – but soon I saw it was only a passion that had moved into his body, like a stranger. (**Alfieri** *pauses, looks down at his desk, then to* **Eddie** *as though he were continuing a conversation with him.*) I don't quite understand what I can do for you. Is there a question of law somewhere?

Eddie   That's what I want to ask you.

Alfieri   Because there's nothing illegal about a girl falling in love with an immigrant.

Eddie   Yeah, but what about it if the only reason for it is to get his papers?

Alfieri   First of all you don't know that.

Eddie   I see it in his eyes; he's laughin' at her and he's laughin' at me.

Alfieri   Eddie, I'm a lawyer. I can only deal in what's provable. You understand that, don't you? Can you prove that?

Eddie   I know what's in his mind, Mr Alfieri!

Alfieri   Eddie, even if you could prove that –

Eddie   Listen . . . will you listen to me a minute? My father always said you was a smart man. I want you to listen to me.

Alfieri   I'm only a lawyer, Eddie.

Eddie   Will you listen a minute? I'm talkin' about the law. Lemme just bring out what I mean. A man, which he comes into the country illegal, don't it stand to reason he's gonna take every penny and put it in the sock? Because they don't know from one day to another, right?

Alfieri   All right.

Eddie   He's spendin'. Records he buys now. Shoes. Jackets. Y'understand me? This guy ain't worried. This guy is *here*. So it must be that he's got it all laid out in his mind already – he's stayin'. Right?

Alfieri   Well? What about it?

Eddie   All right. (*He glances at* **Alfieri**, *then down to the floor.*) I'm talking to you confidential, ain't I?

Alfieri   Certainly.

Eddie   I mean it don't go no place but here. Because I don't like to say this about anybody. Even my wife I didn't exactly say this.

Alfieri   What is it?

Eddie (*takes a breath and glances briefly over each shoulder*)   The guy ain't right, Mr Alfieri.

Alfieri   What do you mean?

Eddie   I mean he ain't right.

Alfieri   I don't get you.

Eddie (*shifts to another position in the chair*)   Dja ever get a look at him?

Alfieri   Not that I know of, no.

Eddie   He's a blond guy. Like . . . platinum. You know what I mean?

Alfieri   No.

Eddie   I mean if you close the paper fast – you could blow him over.

Alfieri   Well that doesn't mean –

Eddie   Wait a minute, I'm tellin' you sump'm. He sings, see. Which is – I mean it's all right, but sometimes he hits a note, see. I turn around. I mean – high. You know what I mean?

Alfieri   Well, that's a tenor.

Eddie   I know a tenor, Mr Alfieri. This ain't no tenor. I mean if you came in the house and you didn't know who was singin', you wouldn't be lookin' for him you be lookin' for her.

Alfieri   Yes, but that's not –

Eddie I'm tellin' you sump'm, wait a minute. Please, Mr Alfieri. I'm tryin' to bring out my thoughts here. Couple of nights ago my niece brings out a dress which it's too small for her, because she shot up like a light this last year. He takes the dress, lays it on the table, he cuts it up; one-two-three, he makes a new dress. I mean he looked so sweet there, like an angel – you could kiss him he was so sweet.

Alfieri Now look, Eddie –

Eddie Mr Alfieri, they're laughin' at him on the piers. I'm ashamed. Paper Doll they call him. Blondie now. His brother thinks it's because he's got a sense of humor, see – which he's got – but that ain't what they're laughin'. Which they're not goin' to come out with it because they know he's my relative, which they have to see me if they make a crack, y'know? But I know what they're laughin' at, and when I think of that guy layin' his hands on her I could – I mean it's eatin' me out, Mr Alfieri, because I struggled for that girl. And now he comes in my house and –

Alfieri Eddie, look – I have my own children. I understand you. But the law is very specific. The law does not . . .

Eddie (*with a fuller flow of indignation*) You mean to tell me that there's no law that a guy which he ain't right can go to work and marry a girl and – ?

Alfieri You have no recourse in the law, Eddie.

Eddie Yeah, but if he ain't right, Mr Alfieri, you mean to tell me –

Alfieri There is nothing you can do, Eddie, believe me.

Eddie Nothin'.

Alfieri Nothing at all. There's only one legal question here.

Eddie What?

Alfieri The manner in which they entered the country. But I don't think you want to do anything about that, do you?

Eddie You mean – ?

Alfieri   Well, they entered illegally.

Eddie   Oh, Jesus, no, I wouldn't do nothin' about that, I mean –

Alfieri   All right, then, let me talk now, eh?

Eddie   Mr Alfieri, I can't believe what you tell me. I mean there must be some kinda law which –

Alfieri   Eddie, I want you to listen to me. (*Pause.*) You know, sometimes God mixes up the people. We all love somebody, the wife, the kids – every man's got somebody that he loves, heh? But sometimes . . . there's too much. You know? There's too much, and it goes where it mustn't. A man works hard, he brings up a child, sometimes it's a niece, sometimes even a daughter, and he never realizes it, but through the years – there is too much love for the daughter, there is too much love for the niece. Do you understand what I'm saying to you?

Eddie (*sardonically*)   What do you mean, I shouldn't look out for her good?

Alfieri   Yes, but these things have to end, Eddie, that's all. The child has to grow up and go away, and the man has to learn to forget. Because after all, Eddie – what other way can it end? (*Pause.*) Let her go. That's my advice. You did your job, now it's her life; wish her luck, and let her go. (*Pause.*) Will you do that? Because there's no law, Eddie; make up your mind to it; the law is not interested in this.

Eddie   You mean to tell me, even if he's a punk? If he's –

Alfieri   There's nothing you can do.

Eddie *stands.*

Eddie   Well, all right, thanks. Thanks very much.

Alfieri   What are you going to do?

Eddie (*with a helpless but ironic gesture*)   What can I do? I'm a patsy, what can a patsy do? I worked like a dog twenty years so a punk could have her, so that's what I done. I mean, in the worst times, in the worst, when there wasn't a ship comin' in the harbor, I didn't stand around lookin' for relief – I hustled. When there was empty piers in Brooklyn I went to Hoboken, Staten Island, the West Side, Jersey, all over – because I made a promise. I took out of my own mouth to give to her. I took out of my wife's mouth. I walked hungry plenty days in this city! (*It begins to break through.*) And now I gotta sit in my own house and look at a son-of-a-bitch punk like that – which he came out of nowhere! I give him my house to sleep! I take the blankets off my bed for him, and he takes and puts his dirty filthy hands on her like a goddam thief!

Alfieri (*rising*)   But, Eddie, she's a woman now.

Eddie   He's stealing from me!

Alfieri   She wants to get married, Eddie. She can't marry you, can she?

Eddie (*furiously*)   What're you talkin' about, marry me! I don't know what the hell you're talkin' about!

Pause.

Alfieri   I gave you my advice, Eddie. That's it.

Eddie *gathers himself. A pause.*

Eddie   Well, thanks. Thanks very much. It just – it's breakin' my heart, y'know. I –

Alfieri   I understand. Put it out of your mind. Can you do that?

Eddie   I'm – (*He feels the threat of sobs, and with a helpless wave.*) I'll see you around. (*He goes out up the right ramp.*)

Alfieri (*sits on desk*)   There are times when you want to spread an alarm, but nothing has happened. I knew, I knew then and there – I could have finished the whole story that afternoon. It wasn't as though there was a mystery to unravel. I could see every step coming, step after step, like a dark figure walking down a hall toward a certain door. I knew where he was heading for, I knew where he was going to end. And I sat here many afternoons asking myself why, being an intelligent man,

I was so powerless to stop it. I even went to a certain old lady in the neighborhood, a very wise old woman, and I told her, and she only nodded, and said, 'Pray for him . . . ' And so I – waited here.

As lights go out on **Alfieri**, *they rise in the apartment where all are finishing dinner.* **Beatrice** *and* **Catherine** *are clearing the table.*

Catherine   You know where they went?

Beatrice   Where?

Catherine   They went to Africa once. On a fishing boat. (**Eddie** *glances at her.*) It's true, Eddie.

Beatrice *exits into the kitchen with dishes.*

Eddie   I didn't say nothin'. (*He goes to his rocker, picks up a newspaper.*)

Catherine   And I was never even in Staten Island.

Eddie (*sitting with the paper*)   You didn't miss nothin'. (*Pause.* **Catherine** *takes dishes out.*) How long that take you, Marco – to get to Africa?

Marco (*rising*)   Oh . . . two days. We go all over.

Rodolpho (*rising*)   Once we went to Yugoslavia.

Eddie (*to* **Marco**)   They pay all right on them boats?

Beatrice *enters. She and* **Rodolpho** *stack the remaining dishes.*

Marco   If they catch fish they pay all right. (*Sits on a stool.*)

Rodolpho   They're family boats, though. And nobody in our family owned one. So we only worked when one of the families was sick.

Beatrice   Y'know, Marco, what I don't understand – there's an ocean full of fish and yiz are all starvin'.

Eddie   They gotta have boats, nets, you need money.

Catherine *enters.*

Beatrice   Yeah, but couldn't they like fish from the beach? You see them down Coney Island –

Marco   Sardines.

Eddie   Sure. (*Laughing.*) How you gonna catch sardines on a hook?

Beatrice   Oh, I didn't know they're sardines. (*To* **Catherine**.) They're sardines!

Catherine   Yeah, they follow them all over the ocean, Africa, Yugoslavia . . . (*She sits and begins to look through a movie magazine.* **Rodolpho** *joins her.*)

Beatrice (*to* **Eddie**)   It's funny, y'know. You never think of it, that sardines are swimming in the ocean! (*She exits to kitchen with dishes.*)

Catherine   I know. It's like oranges and lemons on a tree. (*To* **Eddie**.) I mean you ever think of oranges and lemons on a tree?

Eddie   Yeah, I know. It's funny. (*To* **Marco**.) I heard that they paint the oranges to make them look orange.

Beatrice *enters.*

Marco (*he has been reading a letter*)   Paint?

Eddie   Yeah, I heard that they grow like green.

Marco   No, in Italy the oranges are orange.

Rodolpho   Lemons are green.

Eddie (*resenting his instruction*)   I know lemons are green, for Christ's sake, you see them in the store they're green sometimes. I said oranges they paint, I didn't say nothin' about lemons.

Beatrice (*sitting; diverting their attention*)   Your wife is gettin' the money all right, Marco?

Marco   Oh, yes. She bought medicine for my boy.

Beatrice   That's wonderful. You feel better, heh?

Marco   Oh, yes! But I'm lonesome.

Beatrice   I just hope you ain't gonna do like some of them around here. They're here twenty-five years, some men, and they didn't get enough together to go back twice.

Marco   Oh, I know. We have many families in our town, the children never saw the father. But I will go home. Three, four years, I think.

Beatrice   Maybe you should keep more here. Because maybe she thinks it comes so easy you'll never get ahead of yourself.

Marco   Oh, no, she saves. I send everything. My wife is very lonesome. (*He smiles shyly.*)

Beatrice   She must be nice. She pretty? I bet, heh?

Marco (*blushing*)   No, but she understand everything.

Rodolpho   Oh, he's got a clever wife!

Eddie   I betcha there's plenty surprises sometimes when those guys get back there, heh?

Marco   Surprises?

Eddie (*laughing*)   I mean, you know – they count the kids and there's a couple extra than when they left?

Marco   No – no . . . The women wait, Eddie. Most. Most. Very few surprises.

Rodolpho   It's more strict in our town. (**Eddie** *looks at him now.*) It's not so free.

Eddie (*rises, paces up and down*)   It ain't so free here either, Rodolpho, like you think. I seen greenhorns sometimes get in trouble that way – they think just because a girl don't go around with a shawl over her head that she ain't strict, y'know? Girl don't have to wear black dress to be strict. Know what I mean?

Rodolpho   Well, I always have respect –

Eddie   I know, but in your town you wouldn't just drag off some girl without permission, I mean. (*He turns.*) You know what I mean, Marco? It ain't that much different here.

Marco (*cautiously*)   Yes.

Beatrice   Well, he didn't exactly drag her off though, Eddie.

Eddie   I know, but I seen some of them get the wrong idea sometimes. (*To* **Rodolpho**.) I mean it might be a little more free here but it's just as strict.

Rodolpho   I have respect for her, Eddie. I do anything wrong?

Eddie   Look, kid, I ain't her father, I'm only her uncle –

Beatrice   Well then, be an uncle then. (**Eddie** *looks at her, aware of her criticizing force.*) I *mean*.

Marco   No, Beatrice, if he does wrong you must tell him. (*To* **Eddie**.) What does he do wrong?

Eddie   Well, Marco, till he came here she was never out on the street twelve o'clock at night.

Marco (*to* **Rodolpho**)   You come home early now.

Beatrice (*to* **Catherine**)   Well, you said the movie ended late, didn't you?

Catherine   Yeah.

Beatrice   Well, tell him, honey. (*To* **Eddie**.) The movie ended late.

Eddie   Look, B, I'm just sayin' – he thinks she always stayed out like that.

Marco   You come home early now, Rodolpho.

Rodolpho (*embarrassed*)   All right, sure. But I can't stay in the house all the time, Eddie.

Eddie   Look, kid, I'm not only talkin' about her. The more you run around like that the more chance you're takin'. (*To* **Beatrice**.) I mean suppose he gets hit by a car or something. (*To* **Marco**.) Where's his papers, who is he? Know what I mean?

Beatrice   Yeah, but who is he in the daytime, though? It's the same chance in the daytime.

Eddie (*holding back a voice full of anger*)   Yeah, but he don't have to go lookin' for it, Beatrice. If he's here to work, then he should work; if he's here for a good time then he could fool around! (*To* **Marco**.) But I understood, Marco, that you was both comin' to make a livin' for your family. You understand me, don't you, Marco? (*He goes to his rocker.*)

Marco   I beg your pardon, Eddie.

Eddie   I mean, that's what I understood in the first place, see.

Marco   Yes. That's why we came.

Eddie (*sits on his rocker*)   Well, that's all I'm askin'.

Eddie *reads his paper. There is a pause, an awkwardness. Now* **Catherine** *gets up and puts a record on the phonograph – 'Paper Doll'.*

Catherine (*flushed with revolt*)   You wanna dance, Rodolpho?

Eddie *freezes.*

Rodolpho (*in deference to* **Eddie**)   No, I – I'm tired.

Beatrice   Go ahead, dance, Rodolpho.

Catherine   Ah, come on. They got a beautiful quartet, these guys. Come.

She has taken his hand and he stiffly rises, feeling **Eddie**'s *eyes on his back, and they dance.*

Eddie (*to* **Catherine**)   What's that, a new record?

Catherine   It's the same one. We bought it the other day.

Beatrice (*to* **Eddie**)   They only bought three records. (*She watches them dance;* **Eddie** *turns his head away.* **Marco** *just sits there, waiting. Now* **Beatrice** *turns to* **Eddie**.) Must be nice to go all over in one of them fishin' boats. I would like that myself. See all them other countries?

Eddie   Yeah.

Beatrice (*to* **Marco**)   But the women don't go along, I bet.

Marco   No, not on the boats. Hard work.

Beatrice   What're you got, a regular kitchen and everything?

Marco   Yes, we eat very good on the boats – especially when Rodolpho comes along; everybody gets fat.

Beatrice   Oh, he cooks?

Marco   Sure, very good cook. Rice, pasta, fish, everything.

Eddie *lowers his paper.*

Eddie   He's a cook, too! (*Looking at* **Rodolpho**.) He sings, he cooks . . .

Rodolpho *smiles thankfully.*

Beatrice   Well it's good, he could always make a living.

Eddie   It's wonderful. He sings, he cooks, he could make dresses . . .

Catherine   They get some high pay, them guys. The head chefs in all the big hotels are men. You read about them.

Eddie   That's what I'm sayin'.

Catherine *and* **Rodolpho** *continue dancing.*

Catherine   Yeah, well, I mean.

Eddie (*to* **Beatrice**)   He's lucky, believe me. (*Slight pause. He looks away, then back to* **Beatrice**.) That's why the water front is no place for him. (*They stop dancing.* **Rodolpho** *turns off phonograph.*) I mean like me – I can't cook, I can't sing, I can't make dresses, so I'm on the water front. But if I could cook, if I could sing, if I could make dresses, I wouldn't be on the water front. (*He has been unconsciously twisting the newspaper into a tight roll. They are all regarding him now; he senses he is exposing the issue and he is driven on.*) I would be someplace else. I would be like in a dress store. (*He has bent the rolled paper and it suddenly tears in two. He suddenly gets up and pulls his pants up over his belly and goes* *to* **Marco**.) What do you, say, Marco, we go to the bouts next Saturday night. You never seen a fight, did you?

Marco (*uneasily*)   Only in the moving pictures.

Eddie (*going to* **Rodolpho**)   I'll treat yiz. What do you say, Danish? You wanna come along? I'll buy the tickets.

Rodolpho   Sure. I like to go.

Catherine (*goes to* **Eddie**; *nervously happy now*)   I'll make some coffee, all right?

Eddie   Go ahead, make some! Make it nice and strong. (*Mystified, she smiles and exits to kitchen. He is weirdly elated, rubbing his fists into his palms. He strides to* **Marco**.) You wait, Marco, you see some real fights here. You ever do any boxing?

Marco   No, I never.

Eddie (*to* **Rodolpho**)   Betcha you have done some, heh?

Rodolpho   No.

Eddie   Well, come on, I'll teach you.

Beatrice   What's he got to learn that for?

Eddie   Ya can't tell, one a these days somebody's liable to step on his foot or sump'm. Come on, Rodolpho, I show you a couple a passes. (*He stands below table.*)

Beatrice   Go ahead, Rodolpho. He's a good boxer, he could teach you.

Rodolpho (*embarrassed*)   Well, I don't know how to – (*He moves down to* **Eddie**.)

Eddie   Just put your hands up. Like this, see? That's right. That's very good, keep your left up, because you lead with the left, see, like this. (*He gently moves his left into* **Rodolpho**'s *face.*) See? Now what you gotta do is you gotta block me, so when I come in like that you – (**Rodolpho** *parries his left.*) Hey, that's very good! (**Rodolpho** *laughs.*) All right, now come into me. Come on.

Rodolpho   I don't want to hit you, Eddie.

Eddie   Don't pity me, come on. Throw it, I'll show you how to block it. (**Rodolpho** *jabs at him, laughing. The others join.*) 'At's it. Come on again. For the jaw right here. (**Rodolpho** *jabs with more assurance.*) Very good!

Beatrice (*to* **Marco**)   He's very good!

Eddie *crosses directly upstage of* **Rodolpho**.

Eddie   Sure, he's great! Come on, kid, put sump'm behind it, you can't hurt me. (**Rodolpho**, *more seriously, jabs at* **Eddie**'s *jaw and grazes it.*) Attaboy.

Catherine *comes from the kitchen, watches.*

Eddie   Now I'm gonna hit you, so block me, see?

Catherine (*with beginning alarm*)   What are they doin'?

They are lightly boxing now.

Beatrice (*she senses only the comradeship in it now*)   He's teachin' him; he's very good!

Eddie   Sure, he's terrific! Look at him go! (**Rodolpho** *lands a blow.*) 'At's it! Now, watch out, here I come, Danish! (*He feints with his left hand and lands with his right. It mildly staggers* **Rodolpho**. **Marco** *rises.*)

Catherine (*rushing to* **Rodolpho**)   Eddie!

Eddie   Why? I didn't hurt him. Did I hurt you, kid? (*He rubs the back of his hand across his mouth.*)

Rodolpho   No, no, he didn't hurt me. (*To* **Eddie** *with a certain gleam and a smile.*) I was only surprised.

Beatrice (*pulling* **Eddie** *down into the rocker*)   That's enough, Eddie; he did pretty good though.

Eddie   Yeah. (*Rubbing his fists together.*) He could be very good, Marco. I'll teach him again.

Marco *nods at him dubiously.*

Rodolpho   Dance, Catherine. Come. (*He takes her hand; they go to phonograph and start it. It plays 'Paper Doll'.*)

Rodolpho *takes her in his arms. They dance.* **Eddie** *in thought sits in his chair, and* **Marco** *takes a chair, places it in front of* **Eddie**, *and looks down at it.* **Beatrice** *and* **Eddie** *watch him.*

Marco   Can you lift this chair?

Eddie   What do you mean?

Marco   From here. (*He gets on one knee with one hand behind his back, and grasps the bottom of one of the chair legs but does not raise it.*)

Eddie   Sure, why not? (*He comes to the chair, kneels, grasps the leg, raises the chair one inch, but it leans over to the floor.*) Gee, that's hard, I never knew that. (*He tries again, and again fails.*) It's on an angle, that's why, heh?

Marco   Here. (*He kneels, grasps, and with strain slowly raises the chair higher and higher, getting to his feet now.* **Rodolpho** *and* **Catherine** *have stopped dancing as* **Marco** *raises the chair over his head.*)

Marco *is face to face with* **Eddie**, *a strained tension gripping his eyes and jaw, his neck stiff, the chair raised like a weapon over* **Eddie**'s *head – and he transforms what might appear like a glare of warning into a smile of triumph, and* **Eddie**'s *grin vanishes as he absorbs his look.*

Curtain.

Act Two

Light rises on **Alfieri** *at his desk.*

Alfieri   On the twenty-third of that December a case of
Scotch whisky slipped from a net while being unloaded – as a
case of Scotch whisky is inclined to do on the twenty-third of
December on Pier Forty-one. There was no snow, but it was
cold, his wife was out shopping. Marco was still at work. The
boy had not been hired that day; Catherine told me later that
this was the first time they had been alone together in the house.

Light is rising on **Catherine** *in the apartment.* **Rodolpho** *is
watching as she arranges a paper pattern on cloth spread on the table.*

Catherine   You hungry?

Rodolpho   Not for anything to eat. (*Pause.*) I have nearly
three hundred dollars. Catherine?

Catherine   I heard you.

Rodolpho   You don't like to talk about it any more?

Catherine   Sure, I don't mind talkin' about it.

Rodolpho   What worries you, Catherine?

Catherine   I been wantin' to ask you about something.
Could I?

Rodolpho   All the answers are in my eyes, Catherine. But
you don't look in my eyes lately. You're full of secrets. (*She looks
at him. She seems withdrawn.*) What is the question?

Catherine   Suppose I wanted to live in Italy.

Rodolpho (*smiling at the incongruity*)   You going to marry
somebody rich?

Catherine   No, I mean live there – you and me.

Rodolpho (*his smile vanishing*)   When?

Catherine   Well . . . when we get married.

Rodolpho (*astonished*)   You want to be an Italian?

Catherine   No, but I could live there without being Italian. Americans live there.

Rodolpho   For ever?

Catherine   Yeah.

Rodolpho (*crosses to rocker*)   You're fooling.

Catherine   No, I mean it.

Rodolpho   Where do you get such an idea?

Catherine   Well, you're always saying it's so beautiful there, with the mountains and the ocean and all the –

Rodolpho   You're fooling me.

Catherine   I mean it.

Rodolpho (*goes to her slowly*)   Catherine, if I ever brought you home with no money, no business, nothing, they would call the priest and the doctor and they would say Rodolpho is crazy.

Catherine   I know, but I think we would be happier there.

Rodolpho   Happier! What would you eat? You can't cook the view!

Catherine   Maybe you could be a singer, like in Rome or –

Rodolpho   Rome! Rome is full of singers.

Catherine   Well, I could work then.

Rodolpho   Where?

Catherine   God, there must be jobs somewhere!

Rodolpho   There's nothing! Nothing, nothing, nothing. Now tell me what you're talking about. How can I bring you from a rich country to suffer in a poor country? What are you talking about? (*She searches for words.*) I would be a criminal stealing your face. In two years you would have an old, hungry face. When my brother's babies cry they give them water, water that boiled a bone. Don't you believe that?

Catherine (*quietly*)   I'm afraid of Eddie here.

Slight pause.

Rodolpho (*steps closer to her*)   We wouldn't live here. Once I am
a citizen I could work anywhere and I would find better jobs
and we would have a house, Catherine. If I were not afraid to
be arrested I would start to be something wonderful here!

Catherine (*steeling herself*)   Tell me something. I mean just tell
me, Rodolpho – would you still want to do it if it turned out
we had to go live in Italy? I mean just if it turned out that way.

Rodolpho   This is your question or his question?

Catherine   I would like to know, Rodolpho. I mean it.

Rodolpho   To go there with nothing.

Catherine   Yeah.

Rodolpho   No. (*She looks at him wide-eyed.*) No.

Catherine   You wouldn't?

Rodolpho   No; I will not marry you to live in Italy. I want
you to be my wife, and I want to be a citizen. Tell him that, or
I will. Yes. (*He moves about angrily.*) And tell him also, and tell
yourself, please, that I am not a beggar, and you are not a
horse, a gift, a favor for a poor immigrant.

Catherine   Well, don't get mad!

Rodolpho   I am furious! (*Goes to her.*) Do you think I am so
desperate? My brother is desperate, not me. You think I would
carry on my back the rest of my life a woman I didn't love just
to be an American? It's so wonderful? You think we have no tall
buildings in Italy? Electric lights? No wide streets? No flags?
No automobiles? Only work we don't have. I want to be an
American so I can work, that is the only wonder here – work!
How can you insult me, Catherine?

Catherine   I didn't mean that –

Rodolpho   My heart dies to look at you. Why are you so
afraid of him?

Catherine (*near tears*)   I don't know!

Rodolpho   Do you trust me, Catherine? You?

Catherine   It's only that I – He was good to me, Rodolpho. You don't know him; he was always the sweetest guy to me. Good. He razzes me all the time but he don't mean it. I know. I would just feel ashamed if I made him sad. 'Cause I always dreamt that when I got married he would be happy at the wedding, and laughin' – and now he's – mad all the time and nasty – (*She is weeping.*) Tell him you'd live in Italy – just tell him, and maybe he would start to trust you a little, see? Because I want him to be happy; I mean – I like him, Rodolpho – and I can't stand it!

Rodolpho   Oh, Catherine – oh, little girl.

Catherine   I love you, Rodolpho, I love you.

Rodolpho   Then why are you afraid? That he'll spank you?

Catherine   Don't, don't laugh at me! I've been here all my life . . . Every day I saw him when he left in the morning and when he came home at night. You think it's so easy to turn around and say to a man he's nothin' to you no more?

Rodolpho   I know, but –

Catherine   You don't know; nobody knows! I'm not a baby, I know a lot more than people think I know. Beatrice says to be a woman, but –

Rodolpho   Yes.

Catherine   Then why don't she be a woman? If I was a wife I would make a man happy instead of goin' at him all the time. I can tell a block away when he's blue in his mind and just wants to talk to somebody quiet and nice . . . I can tell when he's hungry or wants a beer before he even says anything. I know when his feet hurt him, I mean I *know* him and now I'm supposed to turn around and make a stranger out of him? I don't know why I have to do that, I mean.

Rodolpho   Catherine. If I take in my hands a little bird. And she grows and wishes to fly. But I will not let her out of

my hands because I love her so much, is that right for me to
do? I don't say you must hate him; but anyway you must go,
mustn't you? Catherine?

Catherine (*softly*)   Hold me.

Rodolpho (*clasping her to him*)   Oh, my little girl.

Catherine   Teach me. (*She is weeping.*) I don't know anything,
teach me, Rodolpho, hold me.

Rodolpho   There's nobody here now. Come inside. Come.
(*He is leading her toward the bedrooms.*) And don't cry any more.

Light rises on the street. In a moment **Eddie** *appears. He is unsteady,
drunk. He mounts the stairs. He enters the apartment, looks around, takes
out a bottle from one pocket, puts it on the table. Then another bottle from
another pocket, and a third from an inside pocket. He sees the pattern and
cloth, goes over to it and touches it, and turns toward upstage.*

Eddie   Beatrice? (*He goes to the open kitchen door and looks in.*)
Beatrice? Beatrice?

Catherine *enters from bedroom; under his gaze she adjusts her dress.*

Catherine   You got home early.

Eddie   Knocked off for Christmas early. (*Indicating the pattern.*)
Rodolpho makin' you a dress?

Catherine   No. I'm makin' a blouse.

Rodolpho *appears in the bedroom doorway.* **Eddie** *sees him and his
arm jerks slightly in shock.* **Rodolpho** *nods to him testingly.*

Rodolpho   Beatrice went to buy presents for her mother.

Pause.

Eddie   Pack it up. Go ahead. Get your stuff and get outa
here. (**Catherine** *instantly turns and walks toward the bedroom, and*
Eddie *grabs her arm.*) Where you goin'?

Catherine (*trembling with fright*)   I think I have to get out of
here, Eddie.

Eddie   No, you ain't goin' nowheres, he's the one.

Catherine   I think I can't stay here no more. (*She frees her arm, steps back toward the bedroom.*) I'm sorry, Eddie. (*She sees the tears in his eyes.*) Well, don't cry. I'll be around the neighborhood; I'll see you. I just can't stay here no more. You know I can't. (*Her sobs of pity and love for him break her composure.*) Don't you know I can't? You know that, don't you? (*She goes to him.*) Wish me luck. (*She clasps her hands prayerfully.*) Oh, Eddie, don't be like that!

Eddie   You ain't goin' nowheres.

Catherine   Eddie, I'm not gonna be a baby any more! You –

He reaches out suddenly, draws her to him, and as she strives to free herself he kisses her on the mouth.

Rodolpho   Don't! (*He pulls on **Eddie**'s arm.*) Stop that! Have respect for her!

Eddie (*spun round by **Rodolpho***)   You want something?

Rodolpho   Yes! She'll be my wife. That is what I want. My wife!

Eddie   But what're you gonna be?

Rodolpho   I show you what I be!

Catherine   Wait outside; don't argue with him!

Eddie   Come on, show me! What're you gonna be? Show me!

Rodolpho (*with tears of rage*)   Don't say that to me!

Rodolpho *flies at him in attack.* **Eddie** *pins his arms, laughing, and suddenly kisses him.*

Catherine   Eddie! Let go, ya hear me! I'll kill you! Leggo of him!

*She tears at **Eddie**'s face and **Eddie** releases **Rodolpho**. **Eddie** stands there with tears rolling down his face as he laughs mockingly at **Rodolpho**. She is staring at him in horror. **Rodolpho** is rigid. They are like animals that have torn at one another and broken up without a decision, each waiting for the other's mood.*

Eddie (*to **Catherine***)   You see? (*To **Rodolpho**.*) I give you till tomorrow, kid. Get outa here. Alone. You hear me? Alone.

Catherine   I'm going with him, Eddie. (*She starts toward* **Rodolpho**.)

Eddie (*indicating* **Rodolpho** *with his head*)   Not with that. (*She halts, frightened. He sits, still panting for breath, and they watch him helplessly as he leans toward them over the table.*) Don't make me do nuttin', Catherine. Watch your step, submarine. By rights they oughta throw you back in the water. But I got pity for you. (*He moves unsteadily toward the door, always facing* **Rodolpho**.) Just get outa here and don't lay another hand on her unless you wanna go out feet first. (*He goes out of the apartment.*)

The lights go down, as they rise on **Alfieri**.

Alfieri   On December twenty-seventh I saw him next. I normally go home well before six, but that day I sat around looking out my window at the bay, and when I saw him walking through my doorway, I knew why I had waited. And if I seem to tell this like a dream, it was that way. Several moments arrived in the course of the two talks we had when it occurred to me how – almost transfixed I had come to feel. I had lost my strength somewhere. (**Eddie** *enters, removing his cap, sits in the chair, looks thoughtfully out.*) I looked in his eyes more than I listened – in fact, I can hardly remember the conversation. But I will never forget how dark the room became when he looked at me; his eyes were like tunnels. I kept wanting to call the police, but nothing had happened. Nothing at all had really happened. (*He breaks off and looks down at the desk. Then he turns to* **Eddie**.) So in other words, he won't leave?

Eddie   My wife is talkin' about renting a room upstairs for them. An old lady on the top floor is got an empty room.

Alfieri   What does Marco say?

Eddie   He just sits there. Marco don't say much.

Alfieri   I guess they didn't tell him, heh? What happened?

Eddie   I don't know; Marco don't say much.

Alfieri   What does your wife say?

Eddie (*unwilling to pursue this*) Nobody's talkin' much in the house. So what about that?

Alfieri But you didn't prove anything about him. It sounds like he just wasn't strong enough to break your grip.

Eddie I'm tellin' you I know – he ain't right. Somebody that don't want it can break it. Even a mouse, if you catch a teeny mouse and you hold it in your hand, that mouse can give you the right kind of fight. He didn't give me the right kind of fight, I know it, Mr Alfieri, the guy ain't right.

Alfieri What did you do that for, Eddie?

Eddie To show her what he is! So she would see, once and for all! Her mother'll turn over in the grave! (*He gathers himself almost peremptorily.*) So what do I gotta do now? Tell me what to do.

Alfieri She actually said she's marrying him?

Eddie She told me, yeah. So what do I do?

Slight pause.

Alfieri This is my last word, Eddie, take it or not, that's your business. Morally and legally you have no rights, you cannot stop it; she is a free agent.

Eddie (*angering*) Didn't you hear what I told you?

Alfieri (*with a tougher tone*) I heard what you told me, and I'm telling you what the answer is. I'm not only telling you now, I'm warning you – the law is nature. The law is only a word for what has a right to happen. When the law is wrong it's because it's unnatural, but in this case it is natural and a river will drown you if you buck it now. Let her go. And bless her. (*A phone booth begins to glow on the opposite side of the stage; a faint, lonely blue.* **Eddie** *stands up, jaws clenched.*) Somebody had to come for her, Eddie, sooner or later. (**Eddie** *starts turning to go and* **Alfieri** *rises with new anxiety.*) You won't have a friend in the world, Eddie! Even those who understand will turn against you, even the ones who feel the same will despise you! (**Eddie** *moves off.*)

Put it out of your mind! Eddie! (*He follows into the darkness, calling desperately.*)

Eddie *is gone. The phone is glowing in light now. Light is out on* **Alfieri**. **Eddie** *has at the same time appeared beside the phone.*

Eddie   Give me the number of the Immigration Bureau. Thanks. (*He dials.*) I want to report something. Illegal immigrants. Two of them. That's right. Four-forty-one Saxon Street, Brooklyn, yeah. Ground floor. Heh? (*With greater difficulty.*) I'm just around the neighborhood, that's all. Heh?

Evidently he is being questioned further, and he slowly hangs up. He leaves the phone just as **Louis** *and* **Mike** *come down the street.*

Louis   Go bowlin', Eddie?

Eddie   No, I'm due home.

Louis   Well, take it easy.

Eddie   I'll see yiz.

They leave him, exiting right, and he watches them go. He glances about, then goes up into the house. The lights go on in the apartment. **Beatrice** *is taking down Christmas decorations and packing them in a box.*

Eddie   Where is everybody? (**Beatrice** *does not answer.*) I says where is everybody?

Beatrice (*looking up at him, wearied with it, and concealing a fear of him*)   I decided to move them upstairs with Mrs Dondero.

Eddie   Oh, they're all moved up there already?

Beatrice   Yeah.

Eddie   Where's Catherine? She up there?

Beatrice   Only to bring pillow cases.

Eddie   She ain't movin' in with them.

Beatrice   Look, I'm sick and tired of it. I'm sick and tired of it!

Eddie   All right, all right, take it easy.

Beatrice   I don't wanna hear no more about it, you understand? Nothin'!

Eddie   What're you blowin' off about? Who brought them in here?

Beatrice   All right, I'm sorry; I wish I'd a drop dead before I told them to come. In the ground I wish I was.

Eddie   Don't drop dead, just keep in mind who brought them in here, that's all. (*He moves about restlessly.*) I mean I got a couple of rights here. (*He moves, wanting to beat down her evident disapproval of him.*) This is my house here not their house.

Beatrice   What do you want from me? They're moved out; what do you want now?

Eddie   I want my respect!

Beatrice   So I moved them out, what more do you want? You got your house now, you got your respect.

Eddie (*he moves about biting his lip*)   I don't like the way you talk to me, Beatrice.

Beatrice   I'm just tellin' you I done what you want!

Eddie   I don't like it! The way you talk to me and the way you look at me. This is my house. And she is my niece and I'm responsible for her.

Beatrice   So that's why you done that to him?

Eddie   I done what to him?

Beatrice   What you done to him in front of her; you know what I'm talkin' about. She goes around shakin' all the time, she can't go to sleep! That's what you call responsible for her?

Eddie (*quietly*)   The guy ain't right, Beatrice. (*She is silent.*) Did you hear what I said?

Beatrice   Look, I'm finished with it. That's all. (*She resumes her work.*)

Eddie (*helping her to pack the tinsel*)   I'm gonna have it out with you one of these days, Beatrice.

Beatrice   Nothin' to have out with me, it's all settled. Now we gonna be like it never happened, that's all.

Eddie   I want my respect, Beatrice, and you know what I'm talkin' about.

Beatrice   What?

Pause.

Eddie (*finally his resolution hardens*)   What I feel like doin' in the bed and what I don't feel like doin'. I don't want no –

Beatrice   When'd I say anything about that?

Eddie   You said, you said, I ain't deaf. I don't want no more conversations about that, Beatrice. I do what I feel like doin' or what I don't feel like doin'.

Beatrice   Okay.

Pause.

Eddie   You used to be different, Beatrice. You had a whole different way.

Beatrice   *I'm* no different.

Eddie   You didn't used to jump me all the time about everything. The last year or two I come in the house I don't know what's gonna hit me. It's a shootin' gallery in here and I'm the pigeon.

Beatrice   Okay, okay.

Eddie   Don't tell me okay, okay, I'm tellin' you the truth. A wife is supposed to believe the husband. If I tell you that guy ain't right don't tell me he is right.

Beatrice   But how do you know?

Eddie   Because I know. I don't go around makin' accusations. He give me the heeby-jeebies the first minute I seen him. And I don't like you sayin' I don't want her marryin' anybody. I broke my back payin' her stenography lessons so she could go out and meet a better class of people. Would I do that if I didn't want her to get married? Sometimes you talk like I was a crazy man or sump'm.

Beatrice   But she likes him.

Eddie   Beatrice, she's a baby, how is she gonna know what she likes?

Beatrice   Well, you kept her a baby, you wouldn't let her go out. I told you a hundred times.

Pause.

Eddie   All right. Let her go out, then.

Beatrice   She don't wanna go out now. It's too late, Eddie.

Pause.

Eddie   Suppose I told her to go out. Suppose I –

Beatrice   They're going to get married next week, Eddie.

Eddie (*his head jerks around to her*)   She said that?

Beatrice   Eddie, if you want my advice, go to her and tell her good luck. I think maybe now that you had it out you learned better.

Eddie   What's the hurry next week?

Beatrice   Well, she's been worried about him bein' picked up; this way he could start to be a citizen. She loves him, Eddie. (*He gets up, moves about uneasily, restlessly.*) Why don't you give her a good word? Because I still think she would like you to be a friend, y'know? (*He is standing, looking at the floor.*) I mean like if you told her you'd go to the wedding.

Eddie   She asked you that?

Beatrice   I know she would like it. I'd like to make a party here for her. I mean there oughta be some kinda send-off. Heh? I mean she'll have trouble enough in her life, let's start it off happy. What do you say? 'Cause in her heart she still loves you, Eddie. I know it. (*He presses his fingers against his eyes.*) What're you, cryin'? (*She goes to him, holds his face.*) Go . . . whyn't you go tell her you're sorry? (**Catherine** *is seen on the upper* *landing of the stairway, and they hear her descending.*) There . . . she's comin' down. Come on, shake hands with her.

Eddie (*moving with suppressed suddenness*)   No, I can't, I can't talk to her.

Beatrice   Eddie, give her a break; a wedding should be happy!

Eddie   I'm goin', I'm goin' for a walk.

He goes upstage for his jacket. **Catherine** *enters and starts for the bedroom door.*

Beatrice   Katie? . . . Eddie, don't go, wait a minute. (*She embraces* **Eddie**'s *arm with warmth.*) Ask him, Katie. Come on, honey.

Eddie   It's all right, I'm – (*He starts to go and she holds him.*)

Beatrice   No, she wants to ask you. Come on, Katie, ask him. We'll have a party! What're we gonna do, hate each other? Come on!

Catherine   I'm gonna get married, Eddie. So if you wanna come, the wedding be on Saturday.

Pause.

Eddie   Okay. I only wanted the best for you, Katie. I hope you know that.

Catherine   Okay. (*She starts out again.*)

Eddie   Catherine? (*She turns to him.*) I was just tellin' Beatrice . . . if you wanna go out, like . . . I mean I realize maybe I kept you home too much. Because he's the first guy you ever knew, y'know? I mean now that you got a job, you might meet some fellas, and you get a different idea, y'know? I mean you could always come back to him, you're still only kids, the both of yiz. What's the hurry? Maybe you'll get around a little bit, you grow up a little more, maybe you'll see different in a couple of months. I mean you be surprised, it don't have to be him.

Catherine   No, we made it up already.

Eddie (*with increasing anxiety*)   Katie, wait a minute.

Catherine   No, I made up my mind.

Eddie   But you never knew no other fella, Katie! How could you make up your mind?

Catherine   'Cause I did. I don't want nobody else.

Eddie   But, Katie, suppose he gets picked up.

Catherine   That's why we gonna do it right away. Soon as we finish the wedding he's goin' right over and start to be a citizen. I made up my mind, Eddie. I'm sorry. (*To* **Beatrice**.) Could I take two more pillow cases for the other guys?

Beatrice   Sure, go ahead. Only don't let her forget where they came from.

Catherine *goes into a bedroom.*

Eddie   She's got other boarders up there?

Beatrice   Yeah, there's two guys that just came over.

Eddie   What do you mean, came over?

Beatrice   From Italy. Lipari the butcher – his nephew. They come from Bari, they just got here yesterday. I didn't even know till Marco and Rodolpho moved up there before. (**Catherine** *enters, going toward exit with two pillow cases.*) It'll be nice, they could all talk together.

Eddie   Catherine! (*She halts near the exit door. He takes in* **Beatrice** *too.*) What're you, got no brains? You put them up there with two other submarines?

Catherine   Why?

Eddie (*in a driving fright and anger*)   Why! How do you know they're not trackin' these guys? They'll come up for them and find Marco and Rodolpho! Get them out of the house!

Beatrice   But they been here so long already –

Eddie   How do you know what enemies Lipari's got? Which they'd love to stab him in the back?

Catherine   Well what'll I do with them?

Eddie   The neighborhood is full of rooms. Can't you stand to live a couple of blocks away from him? Get them out of the house!

Catherine   Well maybe tomorrow night I'll –

Eddie   Not tomorrow, do it now. Catherine, you never mix yourself with somebody else's family! These guys get picked up, Lipari's liable to blame you or me and we got his whole family on our head. They got a temper, that family.

Two men in overcoats appear outside, start into the house.

Catherine   How'm I gonna find a place tonight?

Eddie   Will you stop arguin' with me and get them out! You think I'm always tryin' to fool you or sump'm? What's the matter with you, don't you believe I could think of your good? Did I ever ask sump'm for myself? You think I got no feelin's? I never told you nothin' in my life that wasn't for your good. Nothin'! And look at the way you talk to me! Like I was an enemy! Like I – (*A knock on the door. His head swerves. They all stand motionless. Another knock.* **Eddie**, *in a whisper, pointing upstage.*) Go up the fire escape, get them out over the back fence.

Catherine *stands motionless, uncomprehending.*

First Officer (*in the hall*)   Immigration! Open up in there!

Eddie   Go, go. Hurry up! (*She stands a moment staring at him in a realized horror.*) Well, what're you lookin' at!

First Officer   Open up!

Eddie (*calling toward door*)   Who's that there?

First Officer   Immigration, open up.

Eddie *turns, looks at* **Beatrice**. *She sits. Then he looks at* **Catherine**. *With a sob of fury* **Catherine** *streaks into a bedroom.*

Knock is repeated.

Eddie   All right, take it easy, take it easy. (*He goes and opens the door. The* **Officer** *steps inside.*) What's all this?

First Officer   Where are they?

Second Officer *sweeps past and, glancing about, goes into the kitchen.*

Eddie   Where's who?

First Officer   Come on, come on, where are they? (*He hurries into the bedrooms.*)

Eddie   Who? We got nobody here. (*He looks at* **Beatrice**, *who turns her head away. Pugnaciously, furious, he steps toward* **Beatrice**.) What's the matter with *you*?

First Officer *enters from the bedroom, calls to the kitchen.*

First Officer   Dominick?

Enter **Second Officer** *from kitchen.*

Second Officer   Maybe it's a different apartment.

First Officer   There's only two more floors up there. I'll take the front, you go up the fire escape. I'll let you in. Watch your step up there.

Second Officer   Okay, right, Charley. (**First Officer** *goes out apartment door and runs up the stairs.*) This is Four-forty-one, isn't it?

Eddie   That's right.

Second Officer *goes out into the kitchen.*

Eddie *turns to* **Beatrice**. *She looks at him now and sees his terror.*

Beatrice (*weakened with fear*)   Oh, Jesus, Eddie.

Eddie   What's the matter with *you*?

Beatrice (*pressing her palms against her face*)   Oh, my God, my God . . .

Eddie   What're you, accusin' me?

Beatrice (*her final thrust is to turn toward him instead of running from him*)   My God, what did you do?

Many steps on the outer stair draw his attention. We see the **First Officer** *descending, with* **Marco**, *behind him* **Rodolpho**, *and* **Catherine** *and the two strange immigrants, followed by* **Second Officer**. **Beatrice** *hurries to door.*

Catherine (*backing down stairs, fighting with* **First Officer**; *as they appear on the stairs*)   What do yiz want from them? They work, that's all. They're boarders upstairs, they work on the piers.

Beatrice (*to* **First Officer**)   Ah, Mister, what do you want from them, who do they hurt?

Catherine (*pointing to* **Rodolpho**)   They ain't no submarines, he was born in Philadelphia.

First Officer   Step aside, lady.

Catherine   What do you mean? You can't just come in a house and –

First Officer   All right, take it easy. (*To* **Rodolpho**.) What street were you born in Philadelphia?

Catherine   What do you mean, what street? Could you tell me what street you were born?

First Officer   Sure. Four blocks away, One-eleven Union Street. Let's go fellas.

Catherine (*fending him off* **Rodolpho**)   No, you can't! Now, get outa here!

First Officer   Look, girlie, if they're all right they'll be out tomorrow. If they're illegal they go back where they came from. If you want, get yourself a lawyer, although I'm tellin' you now you're wasting your money. Let's get them in the car, Dom. (*To the men.*) Andiamo, andiamo, let's go.

The men start, but **Marco** *hangs back.*

Beatrice (*from doorway*)   Who're they hurtin', for God's sake, what do you want from them? They're starvin' over there, what do you want! Marco!

Marco *suddenly breaks from the group and dashes into the room and faces* **Eddie;** **Beatrice** *and* **First Officer** *rush in as* **Marco** *spits into* **Eddie**'s *face.*

Catherine *runs into hallway and throws herself into* **Rodolpho**'s *arms.* **Eddie***, with an enraged cry, lunges for* **Marco***.*

Eddie   Oh, you mother's – !

First Officer *quickly intercedes and pushes* **Eddie** *from* **Marco***, who stands there accusingly.*

First Officer (*between them, pushing* **Eddie** *from* **Marco**)   Cut it out!

Eddie (*over the* **First Officer**'s *shoulder, to* **Marco**)   I'll kill you for that, you son of a bitch!

First Officer   Hey! (*Shakes him.*) Stay in here now, don't come out, don't bother him. You hear me? Don't come out, fella.

For an instant there is silence. Then **First Officer** *turns and takes* **Marco**'s *arm and then gives a last, informative look at* **Eddie***. As he and* **Marco** *are going out into the hall.* **Eddie** *erupts.*

Eddie   I don't forget that, Marco! You hear what I'm sayin'?

Out in the hall, **First Officer** *and* **Marco** *go down the stairs. Now, in the street,* **Louis***,* **Mike***. and several neighbors including the butcher,* **Lipari** *– a stout, intense, middle-aged man – are gathering around the stoop.*

Lipari*, the butcher, walks over to the two strange men and kisses them. His wife, keening, goes and kisses their hands.* **Eddie** *is emerging from the house shouting after* **Marco***.* **Beatrice** *is trying to restrain him.*

Eddie   That's the thanks I get? Which I took the blankets off my bed for yiz? You gonna apologize to me, Marco! *Marco!*

First Officer (*in the doorway with* **Marco**)   All right, lady, let them go. Get in the car, fellas, it's right over there.

Rodolpho *is almost carrying the sobbing* **Catherine** *off up the street, left.*

Catherine   He was born in Philadelphia! What do you want from him?

First Officer   Step aside, lady, come on now . . .

*The **Second Officer** has moved off with the two strange men.*

Marco, *taking advantage of the **First Officer**'s being occupied with **Catherine**, suddenly frees himself and points back at **Eddie**.*

Marco   That one! I accuse that one!

Eddie *brushes **Beatrice** aside and rushes out to the stoop.*

First Officer (*grabbing him and moving him quickly off up the left street*)   Come on!

Marco (*as he is taken off, pointing back at **Eddie***)   That one! He killed my children! That one stole the food from my children!

Marco *is gone. The crowd has turned to **Eddie**.*

Eddie (*to **Lipari** and wife*)   He's crazy! I give them the blankets off my bed. Six months I kept them like my own brothers!

Lipari, *the butcher, turns and starts up left with his arm around his wife.*

Eddie   Lipari! (*He follows **Lipari** up left.*) For Christ's sake, I kept them, I give them the blankets off my bed!

Lipari *and wife exit.* **Eddie** *turns and starts crossing down right to **Louis** and **Mike**.*

Eddie   Louis! *Louis!*

Louis *barely turns, then walks off and exits down right with **Mike**. Only **Beatrice** is left on the stoop.* **Catherine** *now returns, blank-eyed, from offstage and the car.* **Eddie** *calls after **Louis** and **Mike**.*

Eddie   He's gonna take that back. He's gonna take that back or I'll kill him! You hear me? I'll kill him! I'll kill him! (*He exits up street calling.*)

There is a pause of darkness before the lights rise, on the reception room of a prison. **Marco** *is seated;* **Alfieri**, **Catherine**, *and* **Rodolpho** *standing.*

Alfieri   I'm waiting, Marco, what do you say?

Rodolpho   Marco never hurt anybody.

Alfieri   I can bail you out until your hearing comes up. But I'm not going to do it, you understand me? Unless I have your promise. You're an honorable man, I will believe your promise. Now what do you say?

Marco   In my country he would be dead now. He would not live this long.

Alfieri   All right, Rodolpho – you come with me now.

Rodolpho   No! Please, mister. Marco – promise the man. Please, I want you to watch the wedding. How can I be married and you're in here? Please, you're not going to do anything; you know you're not.

Marco *is silent.*

Catherine (*kneeling left of* **Marco**)   Marco, don't you understand? He can't bail you out if you're gonna do something bad. To hell with Eddie. Nobody is gonna talk to him again if he lives to a hundred. Everybody knows you spit in his face, that's enough, isn't it? Give me the satisfaction – I want you at the wedding. You got a wife and kids, Marco. You could be workin' till the hearing comes up, instead of layin' around here.

Marco (*to* **Alfieri**)   I have no chance?

Alfieri (*crosses to behind* **Marco**)   No, Marco. You're going back. The hearing is a formality, that's all.

Marco   But him? There is a chance, eh?

Alfieri   When she marries him he can start to become an American. They permit that, if the wife is born here.

Marco (*looking at* **Rodolpho**)   Well – we did something. (*He lays a palm on* **Rodolpho**'s *arm and* **Rodolpho** *covers it.*)

Rodolpho   Marco, tell the man.

Marco (*pulling his hand away*)   What will I tell him? He knows such a promise is dishonorable.

Alfieri   To promise not to kill is not dishonorable.

Marco (*looking at* **Alfieri**)   No?

Alfieri   No.

Marco (*gesturing with his head – this is a new idea*)   Then what is done with such a man?'

Alfieri   Nothing. If he obeys the law, he lives. That's all.

Marco (*rises, turns to* **Alfieri**)   The law? All the law is not in a book.

Alfieri   Yes. In a book. There is no other law.

Marco (*his anger rising*)   He degraded my brother. My blood. He robbed my children, he mocks my work. I work to come here, mister!

Alfieri   I know, Marco –

Marco   There is no law for that? Where is the law for that?

Alfieri   There is none.

Marco (*shaking his head, sitting*)   I don't understand this country.

Alfieri   Well? What is your answer? You have five or six weeks you could work. Or else you sit here. What do you say to me?

Marco (*lowers his eyes. It almost seems he is ashamed*)   All right.

Alfieri   You won't touch him. This is your promise.

Slight pause.

Marco   Maybe he wants to apologize to me.

Marco *is staring away.* **Alfieri** *takes one of his hands.*

Alfieri   This is not God, Marco. You hear? Only God makes justice.

Marco   All right.

Alfieri (*nodding, not with assurance*)   Good! Catherine, Rodolpho, Marco, let us go.

Catherine *kisses* **Rodolpho** *and* **Marco**, *then kisses* **Alfieri**'s *hand.*

Catherine   I'll get Beatrice and meet you at the church. (*She leaves quickly.*)

Marco *rises.* **Rodolpho** *suddenly embraces him.* **Marco** *pats him on the back and* **Rodolpho** *exits after* **Catherine**. **Marco** *faces* **Alfieri**.

Alfieri   Only God, Marco.

Marco *turns and walks out.* **Alfieri** *with a certain processional tread leaves the stage. The lights dim out.*

The lights rise in the apartment. **Eddie** *is alone in the rocker, rocking back and forth in little surges. Pause. Now* **Beatrice** *emerges from a bedroom. She is in her best clothes, wearing a hat.*

Beatrice (*with fear, going to* **Eddie**)   I'll be back in about an hour, Eddie. All right?

Eddie (*quietly, almost inaudibly, as though drained*)   What, have I been talkin' to myself?

Beatrice   Eddie, for God's sake, it's her wedding.

Eddie   Didn't you hear what I told you? You walk out that door to that wedding you ain't comin' back here, Beatrice.

Beatrice   Why! What do you want?

Eddie   I want my respect. Didn't you ever hear of that? From my wife?

Catherine *enters from bedroom.*

Catherine   It's after three; we're supposed to be there already, Beatrice. The priest won't wait.

Beatrice   Eddie. It's her wedding. There'll be nobody there from her family. For my sister let me go. I'm goin' for my sister.

Eddie (*as though hurt*)   Look, I been arguin' with you all day already, Beatrice, and I said what I'm gonna say. He's gonna come here and apologize to me or nobody from this house is goin' into that church today. Now if that's more to you than I am, then go. But don't come back. You be on my side or on their side, that's all.

Catherine (*suddenly*)   Who the hell do you think you are?

Beatrice   Sssh!

Catherine   You got no more right to tell nobody nothin'! Nobody! The rest of your life, nobody!

Beatrice   Shut up, Katie! (*She turns* **Catherine** *around.*)

Catherine   You're gonna come with me!

Beatrice   I can't, Katie, I can't . . .

Catherine   How can you listen to him? This rat!

Beatrice (*shaking* **Catherine**)   Don't you call him that!

Catherine (*clearing from* **Beatrice**)   What're you scared of? He's a rat! He belongs in the sewer!

Beatrice   Stop it!

Catherine (*weeping*)   He bites people when they sleep! He comes when nobody's lookin' and poisons decent people. In the garbage he belongs!

Eddie *seems about to pick up the table and fling it at her.*

Beatrice   No, Eddie! Eddie! (*To* **Catherine**.) Then we all belong in the garbage. You, and me too. Don't say that. Whatever happened we all done it, and don't you ever forget it, Catherine. (*She goes to* **Catherine**.) Now go, go to your wedding, Katie, I'll stay home. Go. God bless you, God bless your children.

Enter **Rodolpho**.

Rodolpho   Eddie?

Eddie   Who said you could come in here? Get outa here!

Rodolpho   Marco is coming, Eddie. (*Pause.* **Beatrice** *raises her hands in terror.*) He's praying in the church. You understand? (*Pause.* **Rodolpho** *advances into the room.*) Catherine, I think it is better we go. Come with me.

Catherine   Eddie, go away please.

Beatrice (*quietly*)   Eddie. Let's go someplace. Come. You and me. (*He has not moved.*) I don't want you to be here when he comes. I'll get your coat.

Eddie   Where? Where am I goin'? This is my house.

Beatrice (*crying out*)   What's the use of it! He's crazy now, you know the way they get, what good is it! You got nothin' against Marco, you always liked Marco!

Eddie   I got nothin' against Marco? Which he called me a rat in front of the whole neighborhood? Which he said I killed his children! Where you been?

Rodolpho (*quite suddenly, stepping up to* **Eddie**)   It is my fault, Eddie. Everything. I wish to apologize. It was wrong that I do not ask your permission. I kiss your hand. (*He reaches for* **Eddie**'s *hand, but* **Eddie** *snaps it away from him.*)

Beatrice   Eddie, he's apologizing!

Rodolpho   I have made all our troubles. But you have insult me too. Maybe God understand why you did that to me. Maybe you did not mean to insult me at all –

Beatrice   Listen to him! Eddie, listen what he's tellin' you!

Rodolpho   I think, maybe when Marco comes, if we can tell him we are comrades now, and we have no more argument between us. Then maybe Marco will not –

Eddie   Now, listen –

Catherine   Eddie, give him a chance!

Beatrice   What do you want! Eddie, what do you want!

Eddie   I want my name! He didn't take my name; he's only a punk. Marco's got my name – (*To* **Rodolpho**.) and you can

run tell him, kid, that he's gonna give it back to me in front
of this neighborhood, or we have it out. (*Hoisting up his pants.*)
Come on, where is he? Take me to him.

Beatrice   Eddie, listen –

Eddie   I heard enough! Come on, let's go!

Beatrice   Only blood is good? He kissed your hand!

Eddie   What he does don't mean nothin' to nobody! (*To*
Rodolpho.) Come on!

Beatrice (*barring his way to the stairs*)   What's gonna mean
somethin'? Eddie, listen to me. Who could give you your name?
Listen to me, I love you, I'm talkin' to you, I love you; if
Marco'll kiss your hand outside, if he goes on his knees, what
is he got to give you? That's not what you want.

Eddie   Don't bother me!

Beatrice   You want somethin' else, Eddie, and you can
never have her!

Catherine (*in horror*)   B!

Eddie (*shocked, horrified, his fists clenching*)   Beatrice!

Marco *appears outside, walking toward the door from a distant point.*

Beatrice (*crying out, weeping*)   The truth is not as bad as
blood, Eddie! I'm tellin' you the truth – tell her goodbye for
ever!

Eddie (*crying out in agony*)   That's what you think of me – that
I would have such thoughts? (*His fists clench his head as though it
will burst.*)

Marco (*calling near the door outside*)   Eddie Carbone!

Eddie *swerves about; all stand transfixed for an instant.*

People appear outside.

Eddie (*as though flinging his challenge*)   Yeah, Marco! Eddie
Carbone. Eddie Carbone. Eddie Carbone. (*He goes up the stairs*

and emerges from the apartment. **Rodolpho** *streaks up and out past him and runs to* **Marco**.)

Rodolpho   No, Marco, please! Eddie, please, he has children! You will kill a family!

Beatrice   Go in the house! Eddie, go in the house!

Eddie (*he gradually comes to address the people*)   Maybe he come to apologize to me. Heh, Marco? For what you said about me in front of the neighborhood? (*He is incensing himself and little bits of laughter even escape him as his eyes are murderous and he cracks his knuckles in his hands with a strange sort of relaxation.*) He knows that ain't right. To do like that? To a man? Which I put my roof over their head and my food in their mouth? Like in the Bible? Strangers I never seen in my whole life? To come out of the water and grab a girl for a passport? To go and take from your own family like from the stable – and never a word to me? And now accusations in the bargain! (*Directly to* **Marco**.) Wipin' the neighborhood with my name like a dirty rag! I want my name, Marco. (*He is moving now, carefully, toward* **Marco**.) Now gimme my name and we go together to the wedding.

Beatrice *and* **Catherine** (*keening*)   Eddie! Eddie, don't! Eddie!

Eddie   No, Marco knows what's right from wrong. Tell the people, Marco, tell them what a liar you are! (*He has his arms spread and* **Marco** *is spreading his.*) Come on, liar, you know what you done! (*He lunges for* **Marco** *as a great hushed shout goes up from the people.*)

Marco *strikes* **Eddie** *beside the neck.*

Marco   Animal! You go on your knees to me!

Eddie *goes down with the blow and* **Marco** *starts to raise a foot to stomp him when* **Eddie** *springs a knife into his hand and* **Marco** *steps back.* **Louis** *rushes in toward* **Eddie**.

Louis   Eddie, for Christ's sake!

Eddie *raises the knife and* **Louis** *halts and steps back.*

Eddie   You lied about me, Marco. Now say it. Come on now, say it!

Marco   Anima-a-a-l!

Eddie *lunges with the knife.* **Marco** *grabs his arm, turning the blade inward and pressing it home as the women and* **Louis** *and* **Mike** *rush in and separate them, and* **Eddie***, the knife still in his hand, falls to his knees before* **Marco***. The two women support him for a moment, calling his name again and again.*

Catherine   Eddie, I never meant to do nothing bad to you.

Eddie   Then why – Oh, B!

Beatrice   Yes, yes!

Eddie   My B!

He dies in her arms, and **Beatrice** *covers him with her body.*

Alfieri*, who is in the crowd, turns out to the audience. The lights have gone down, leaving him in a glow, while behind him the dull prayers of the people and the keening of the women continue.*

Alfieri   Most of the time now we settle for half and I like it better. But the truth is holy, and even as I know how wrong he was, and his death useless, I tremble, for I confess that something perversely pure calls to me from his memory – not purely good, but himself purely, for he allowed himself to be wholly known and for that I think I will love him more than all my sensible clients. And yet, it is better to settle for half, it must be! And so I mourn him – I admit it – with a certain . . . alarm.

Curtain.

Notes

3   *a tenement building*: tenement buildings are of inferior
      quality and located in poor neighbourhoods, typically
      overcrowded and inhabited by the working class. *A View
      from the Bridge* is set in the Brooklyn neighbourhood called
      Red Hook, in the New York harbour south of the
      Brooklyn Bridge. The type of tenement building in Red
      Hook usually contained six to eight family units in three-
      or four-storey structures.

3   *longshoremen*: dockworkers who load and unload cargo from
      ships. Many New York longshoremen were Italian
      immigrants.

3   *pitching coins*: a game played against the wall of a building
      and the pavement.

4   *Al Capone, the greatest Carthagian of them all; Frankie Yale*: Al
      Capone was one of America's best-known Mafia gangsters
      of the 1920s. Although he is associated with the city of
      Chicago, he was born in Brooklyn and he began his
      criminal career in New York. He became part of the
      notorious Five Points gang in Manhattan and worked in the
      gangster Frankie Yale's Coney Island club, the Harvard
      Inn, as a bouncer and bartender. While working at the Inn,
      Capone received his famous facial scars and the nickname
      'Scarface' when he insulted a patron and was attacked by
      her brother. Alfieri calls Al Capone 'The greatest
      Carthagian of all' and he means this to be ironic. Carthage
      was the ancient city located in present-day Tunisia. In the
      first and second centuries BC, it was the centre of a great
      civilisation that fought several wars against Rome.
      Hannibal was a Carthaginian. Sicily, because of its
      proximity to North Africa, was often dominated by the

Carthaginians. Miller compares Carthage's challenges to the Roman Empire to Mafia gangsters like Capone challenging American civil authority.

4   *in some Caesar's year*: under some Roman emperor.

4   *Calabria . . . Syracuse*: Calabria, an impoverished area in southern Italy, was a source of mass migration to the United States. Syracuse, a city on the south-east coast of Sicily, was an important Greek colony and a centre of great theatrical activity.

6   *I promised your mother on her deathbed*: Catherine is the daughter of Nancy, Beatrice's sister. The play is unclear about how she died, but Eddie and Beatrice have raised Catherine since she was a baby.

7   *North River*: another name for the Hudson River on the west of Manhattan.

7   *That's fixed*: Beatrice means this as 'set' or 'determined', but the term also has the connotation of meaning as arranged through illegal activity as 'putting the fix in'.

10   *stenographer*: a boss dictated letters to a stenographer, who wrote them down in shorthand and would then type them up. The stenographer had fewer duties and responsibilities than a secretary.

11   *Navy Yard*: the Brooklyn Navy Yard was the famous shipbuilding yard located on the East River. Arthur Miller worked there during the Second World War before his successful career as a playwright.

13   *Madonna*: Mary, the mother of Jesus Christ. Eddie's description of Catherine as a Madonna has many significant meanings (see 'Language' in Commentary).

14   *We'll bust a bag tomorrow*. Eddie means that a sack of coffee will 'accidentally' get damaged while being unloaded from the ship, enabling him to bring home some of its contents.

14   *Buick*: an American automobile characterised by its large size.

16   *The kid snitched?*: slang for informing. The story about Vinny Bolzano, who informed to immigration authorities, foreshadows Eddie's action.

17   *Captain's pieced off*: slang term for an illegal payment to keep silent.

17   *the Syndicate*: another term for organised crime such as the
      Mafia. Illegal immigrants like Marco and Rodolpho must
      work off the price the Syndicate paid for smuggling them
      into the country.

20   *Danes invaded Sicily*: Sicily, located at the crossroads of the
      Mediterranean, has been one of the most invaded lands
      in Europe. The Viking invasions of Sicily occurred during
      the Middle Ages. This is often used as an explanation for
      the physical appearance of blond, blue-eyed Sicilians.

22   *He trusts his wife*: A reference to the sexual fidelity of Italian
      women. Later in Act One, Eddie implies otherwise.

22   *I understand it's not too good here, either*: A reference to the
      economic conditions and the availability of work in America

25   *Napolidan*: popular Neapolitan songs. *Bel canto*, literally
      'beautiful singing', was a style of singing much favoured
      in mid-nineteenth-century Italy; it emphasised beauty of
      tone in the delivery of highly florid music.

25   *Paper Doll*: the famous hit song by the Mills Brothers.

26   *Garbo*: the Hollywood movie star Greta Garbo.

27   *Paramount*: at the time in which the play is set, New York
      had two movie theatres named the Paramount, one in
      downtown Brooklyn and one in Manhattan.

28   *sump'm*: something.

29   *When am I gonna be a wife again?*: Beatrice and Eddie have
      not had sexual relations in three months.

30   *submarines*: slang for illegal immigrants who have arrived
      by ship, implying the stealthlike way they have arrived in
      America.

30   *Matson Line . . . Moore-MacCormack Line*: names of shipping
      companies.

32   *Times Square*: the famous entertainment centre of New
      York, where Broadway meets Seventh Avenue just north
      of 42nd Street. Tramps in this instance are prostitutes.

32   *Broadway*: the main thoroughfare through Times Square;
      it is the generic name for theatre district in New York.

34   *if you wasn't an orphan, wouldn't he ask your father's permission
      before he run around with you like this?*: Eddie makes a number
      of references to the promise he made to Catherine's
      mother on her deathbed. Note that no mention is made in

the play to Catherine's father. Patriarchal authority remained strong in the 1950s Sicilian-American culture depicted by Miller, and Eddie assumes this role.

34 *Katie, he's only bowin' to his passport*: Eddie insists that Rodolpho only wants to obtain American citizenship, which would be easier for him to achieve if he married an American citizen.

41 *I mean he looked so sweet there, like an angel – you could kiss him he was so sweet*: this line foreshadows the kiss Eddie delivers in Act Two.

41 *There's only one legal question here . . . The manner in which they entered the country. But I don't think you want to do anything about that, do you?*: this foreshadows Eddie's snitching to the immigration authorities, the very act he abhorred earlier in the play.

45 *Coney Island*: the famous amusement park and beach in Brooklyn.

46 *I betcha there's plenty surprises sometimes when those guys get back there, heh?*: Eddie insinuates that many Italian wives are unfaithful to their husbands; consequently, upon his return, a husband may find a child not fathered by him

50 *Danish*: Eddie calls Rodolpho by this name to bring attention again to his unusual blond hair.

55 *This is your question or his question?*: Rodolpho is aware of the doubts which Eddie has placed in Catherine's mind.

56 *razzes*: criticises with the intention of annoying someone.

66 *Bari*: a city on the Adriatic coast in southern Italy.

69 *Andiamo*: 'let's go' in Italian.

70 *Marco spits into Eddie's face* in Italian culture a particularly insulting act.

71 *That one! I accuse that one!* Marco's public accusation humiliates Eddie in front of his neighbours, causing him to be ostracised.

72 *In my country he would be dead now:* Marco seeks the vengeance on Eddie that would be exacted in Italy.

73 *The law? All the law is not in a book:* Marco is frustrated that civil law in America provides no justice for him against Eddie, just as earlier Eddie was frustrated that the law could not help him stop Rodolpho and Catherine's relationship.

Questions for Further Study

1 Discuss Catherine's growing awareness of herself as a woman. Do you think she recognises Eddie's desire for her?

2 How important are Alfieri's roles as lawyer and narrator?

3 Is Eddie a tragic hero? Do we sympathise with him at the play's end?

4 When Miller first heard the tale upon which he based *A View from the Bridge*, he thought it was 'some re-enactment of a Greek myth'. To Miller, the events seemed almost the work of fate. Could Eddie have prevented his fate?

5 Discuss why Alfieri uses the words 'a passion which had moved into Eddie's body'.

6 Rodolpho refuses to go to Italy when he and Catherine marry. Does this give credence to Eddie's claim that Rodolpho is 'bowin' to his passport'?

7 What does the play suggest about immigration issues and illegal aliens?

8 Discuss whether Marco wants to exact justice or revenge on Eddie.

9 Why does Eddie knowingly inform to the immigration authorities when Alfieri has told him the consequences of such an action?

10 Analyse Eddie's apparent lack of awareness of his desire for Catherine.

11 Discuss Eddie's violation of the codes of his society.

12 Explain Eddie's state of mind in wanting his name back. How does he expect to retain his honour in front of his neighbours when he has knowingly informed?

13 How does civil law operate in the play? How does social law operate in the play?

14 The play ends with Eddie crying out, 'My B'. Discuss Beatrice's devotion to Eddie.

15 Discuss the characters in the play who take responsibility for their actions.

16 Analyse Miller's use of symbolic and metaphorical language in the dialogue.

17 Why is the stage presence of the neighbours in the Red Hook community so important to the effect of the play?

18 At the end of the play, Alfieri tells the audience that he mourns Eddie with a 'certain alarm'. Arthur Miller said that Eddie is 'not a man to weep over'. How do you ultimately judge Eddie? What do his actions suggest about the human condition?

19 Discuss how the casting of the play with additional actors affects the production and ultimately the meaning of the play in performance.

20 In the 1956 production of *A View from the Bridge*, the set was more realistic than the skeletal set of the original New York production. Other recent productions of the play have used a scrim of the Brooklyn Bridge and the Brooklyn Navy Yard as backgrounds. Discuss how the set of a particular production can affect the performance of *A View from the Bridge*. How would you design a set for the play?

21 There is significant argument about the meaning of Eddie kissing both Catherine and Rodolpho in Act Two. As a director, how would you block this scene?

22 At the climax of the play, Marco comes to take revenge on Eddie, but it is Eddie who springs the knife on Marco. How does the staging of this scene affect the audience's perception of Eddie's tragedy?

STEPHEN MARINO is founding editor of the *Arthur Miller Journal* and adjunct professor of English at St Francis College, Brooklyn Heights, New York. He is former president of the Arthur Miller Society. His work on Arthur Miller has appeared in *Modern Drama*, the *South Atlantic Review*, the *Nevada Historical Quarterly* and the *Dictionary of Literary Biography*. He is editor of *The Salesman Has a Birthday: Essays Celebrating the Fiftieth Anniversary of Arthur Miller's 'Death of a Salesman'* (University Press of America, 2000) and author of *A Language Study of Arthur Miller's Plays: The Poetic in the Colloquial* (Edwin Mellen Press, 2002). He has also contributed an essay on Miller's poetic language to a collection of essays about Arthur Miller, *Critical Insights* (Salem Press, 2010).

ENOCH BRATER is the Kenneth T. Rowe Collegiate Professor of Dramatic Literature at the University of Michigan. He has published widely in the field of modern drama, and is an internationally renowned expert on such figures as Samuel Beckett and Arthur Miller. His recent books include *Arthur Miller: A Playwright's Life and Works*, *Arthur Miller's America: Theater and Culture in a Time of Change* and *Arthur Miller's Global Theater: How an American Playwright Is Performed on Stages around the World*.